AMERICAN EMPOWER

STUDENT'S BOOK B
WITH DIGITAL PACK

T0349634

B2
UPPER INTERMEDIATE

Adrian Doff, Craig Thaine
Herbert Puchta, Jeff Stranks, Peter Lewis-Jones

CAMBRIDGE

AMERICAN EMPOWER is a six-level general English course for adult and young adult learners, taking students from beginner to advanced level (CEFR A1 to C1). *American Empower* combines course content from Cambridge University Press with validated assessment from the experts at Cambridge Assessment English.

American Empower's unique mix of engaging classroom materials and reliable assessment enables learners to make consistent and measurable progress.

Content you'll love.
Assessment you
can trust.

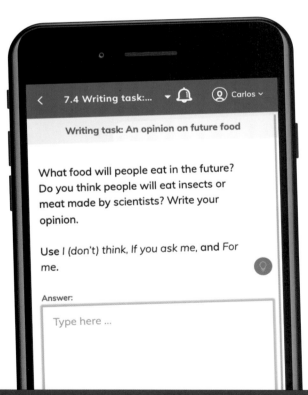

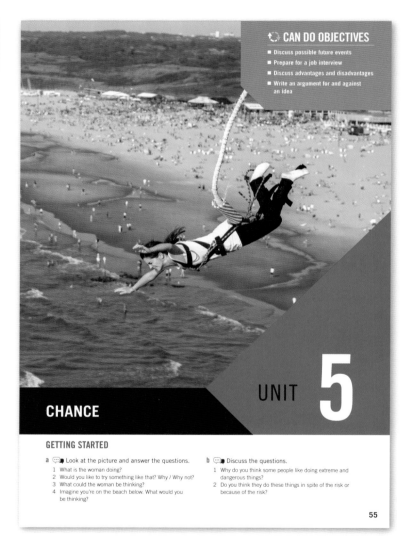

Better Learning with *American Empower*

Better Learning is our simple approach where **insights** we've gained from research have helped shape **content** that drives **results**.

Learner engagement

1 Content that informs and motivates

Insights
Sustained motivation is key to successful language learning and skills development.

Content
Clear learning goals, thought-provoking images, texts, and speaking activities, plus video content to arouse curiosity.

Results
Content that surprises, entertains, and provokes an emotional response, helping teachers to deliver motivating and memorable lessons.

5A | YOU COULD LIVE TO BE A HUNDRED

Learn to discuss possible future events
G Future probability
V Adjectives describing attitude

1 SPEAKING

Are you an OPTIMIST or a PESSIMIST?

a Are you an optimist or a pessimist? Mark your place on this scale, then compare with others in your group.

Optimist ⟷ Pessimist

b Decide what you think about the questions, then compare your answers.

1 If you take a test at the end of this class, how well will you do?

I'll get a perfect score. ⟷ I'll probably fail.

2 Do you expect the coming week to be … ?

exciting/great ⟷ boring/terrible

3 Imagine you left your bag on the bus. Do you expect to get it back?

Yes ⟷ No

4 You start a new workout routine and you're really tired the next day. Do you expect it to be easier the next time?

Yes ⟷ No

c ≫ Communication 5A Now go to p. 129.

d Based on your answers in 1b, decide who in your group … ?
- is the most optimistic
- is the most pessimistic
- is the most realistic

e Write a question to find out if other students are optimistic or pessimistic. Add a) and b) answer choices.

Example:
You want to buy a shirt you like, but the store is sold out. What do you think?
a) I'm sure I can find it somewhere else.
b) Why am I always so unlucky?

WHY WE THINK WE'RE GOING TO HAVE A LONG AND HAPPY LIFE

Researchers have found that people all over the world share an important characteristic: optimism. Sue Reynolds explains what it's all about.

WE'RE ALL ABOVE AVERAGE!
Try asking a 20-year-old these questions:
- What kind of career will you have?
- How long do you think you'll live?

Most people think they'll be able to earn above-average salaries, but only some of the population can make that much. Most young men in Europe will say they expect to live well into their 80s, but the average life expectancy for European men is 75. Most people will give an answer that is unrealistic because nearly everyone believes they will be better than the average. Obviously, they can't all be right.

Most people are also optimistic about their own strengths and abilities. Ask people, "How well do you get along with other people?" or "How intelligent are the people in your family?" and they'll usually say they're above average. Again, they can't all be right. We can't all be better than everyone else, but that's what we think.

LOOKING ON THE BRIGHT SIDE
There is a reason for this. Research has shown that, on the whole, we are optimistic by nature and have a positive view of ourselves. In fact, we are much more optimistic than realistic and frequently imagine things will turn out better than they actually do. Most people don't expect their marriages to end in divorce, they don't expect to lose their jobs, or to be diagnosed with a life-threatening disease. Furthermore, when things do go wrong, they are often quick to find something positive in all the gloom. Many people who fail exams, for example, are convinced they were just unlucky with the questions and they'll do better next time. Or people who have had a serious illness often say that it was really positive because it made them appreciate life more. We really are very good at "looking on the bright side."

THE OPTIMISM BIAS
This certainty that our future is bound to be better than our past and present is known as the "Optimism Bias," and researchers have found that it is common to people all over the world and of all ages. Of course, the Optimism Bias can lead us to make some very bad decisions. Often, people don't take out travel insurance because they're sure everything will be all right, they don't worry about saving up for old age because the future looks fine, or they smoke cigarettes in spite of the health warnings on the pack because they believe "It won't happen to me." Or on a global scale, we keep polluting the planet because we're sure that we'll find a way to clean it up some day in the future.

OPTIMISM IS GOOD FOR YOU
But researchers believe that the Optimism Bias is actually good for us. People who expect the best are generally likely to be ambitious and adventurous, whereas people who expect the worst are likely to be more cautious, so optimism actually helps to make us successful. Optimists are also healthier because they feel less stress – they can relax because they think that everything is going to be just fine. Not only that, but the Optimism Bias may also have played an important part in our evolution as human beings. Because we hoped for the best, we were prepared to take risks such as hunting down dangerous animals and traveling across the sea to find new places to live, and this is why we became so successful as a species. Even if our optimism is unrealistic and leads us to take risks, without it we might all still be living in caves, too afraid to go outside and explore the world in case we get eaten by wild animals.

Even if our optimism is unrealistic and leads us to take risks, without it we might all still be living in caves …

… we keep polluting the planet because we're sure that we'll find a way to clean it up some day …

UNIT 5

2 READING

a Read the article "Why We Think We're Going to Have a Long and Happy Life" quickly. Choose the correct words to complete the summary.
Most people are naturally optimistic / pessimistic, and this is generally an advantage / a disadvantage for the human race because it helps us to be realistic about the future / more successful.

b Read the article again. Check (✓) the five points made in the article.
1 ☐ Pessimists usually have fewer friends than optimists.
2 ☐ Humans are naturally positive about their future.
3 ☐ Reality is often worse than we imagine it to be.
4 ☐ People who live in warmer countries are usually more optimistic.
5 ☐ We often act (or don't act) because we're confident everything will work out.
6 ☐ If we imagine a better future, we will take more risks.
7 ☐ Optimists spend a lot of time daydreaming.
8 ☐ Optimism about the future makes us feel better in the present.

c Discuss the questions.
- Look again at your answers in 1b. Do you think you have the "Optimism Bias"?
- Do you agree that it's better to be optimistic than realistic? Why / Why not?
- How do you see yourself 20 years from now?

3 VOCABULARY
Adjectives describing attitude

a Find adjectives in "Why We Think We're Going to Have a Long and Happy Life" that mean:
1 expecting the future to be good
2 seeing things as they are
3 not seeing things as they are
4 prepared to take risks
5 not prepared to take risks
6 wanting to be successful

b Which of these adjectives best describe you?

c ≫ Now go to Vocabulary Focus 5A on p. 158.

Many people who fail exams are convinced they were just unlucky with the questions …

56 / 57

---

2 Personalized and relevant

Insights
Language learners benefit from frequent opportunities to personalize their responses.

Content
Personalization tasks in every unit make the target language more meaningful to the individual learner.

Results
Personal responses make learning more memorable and inclusive, with all students participating in spontaneous spoken interaction.

Measurable progress

1 Assessment you can trust

Insights
Tests developed and validated by Cambridge Assessment English, the world leaders in language assessment, to ensure they are accurate and meaningful.

Content
End-of-unit tests, mid- and end-of-course competency tests, and personalized CEFR test report forms provide reliable information on progress with language skills.

Results
Teachers can see learners' progress at a glance, and learners can see measurable progress, which leads to greater motivation.

Results of an impact study showing % improvement of Reading levels, based on global *Empower* students' scores over one year.

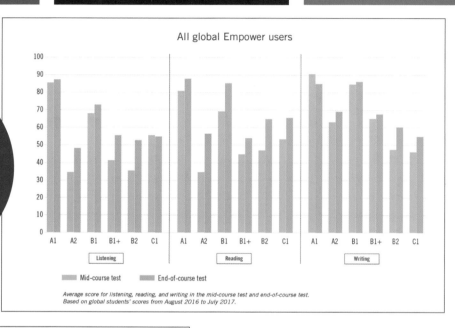

All global Empower users

Mid-course test | End-of-course test

Average score for listening, reading, and writing in the mid-course test and end-of-course test. Based on global students' scores from August 2016 to July 2017.

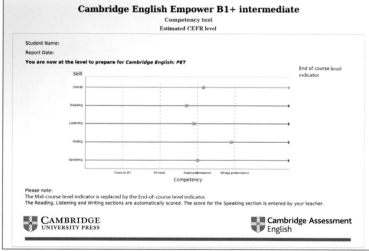

Cambridge English Empower B1+ intermediate
Competency test
Estimated CEFR level

Student Name:
Report Date:

You are now at the level to prepare for *Cambridge English: PET*

Please note:
The Mid-course level indicator is replaced by the End-of-course level indicator.
The Reading, Listening and Writing sections are automatically scored. The score for the Speaking section is entered by your teacher.

CAMBRIDGE UNIVERSITY PRESS   Cambridge Assessment English

> " *We started using the tests provided with* Empower *and our students started showing better results from this point until now.* "
>
> **Kristina Ivanova, Director of Foreign Language Training Centre, ITMO University, Saint Petersburg, Russia**

2 Evidence of impact

Insights
Schools and colleges need to show that they are evaluating the effectiveness of their language programs.

Content
Empower (British English) impact studies have been carried out in various countries, including Russia, Brazil, Turkey, and the UK, to provide evidence of positive impact and progress.

Results
Colleges and universities have demonstrated a significant improvement in language level between the mid- and end-of-course tests, as well as a high level of teacher satisfaction with *Empower*.

Manageable learning

1 Mobile friendly

Insights
Learners expect online content to be mobile friendly but also flexible and easy to use on any digital device.

Content
American Empower provides easy access to Digital Workbook content that works on any device and includes practice activities with audio.

Results
Digital Workbook content is easy to access anywhere, and produces meaningful and actionable data so teachers can track their students' progress and adapt their lesson accordingly.

> **"** *I had been studying English for 10 years before university, and I didn't succeed. But now with Empower I know my level of English has changed.* **"**
>
> **Nikita, *Empower* Student, ITMO University, Saint Petersburg, Russia**

2 Corpus-informed

Insights
Corpora can provide valuable information about the language items learners are able to learn successfully at each CEFR level.

Content
Two powerful resources – Cambridge Corpus and English Profile – informed the development of the *Empower* course syllabus and the writing of the materials.

Results
Learners are presented with the target language they are able to incorporate and use at the right point in their learning journey. They are not overwhelmed with unrealistic learning expectations.

Rich in practice

1 Language in use

Insights
It is essential that learners are offered frequent and manageable opportunities to practice the language they have been focusing on.

Content
Throughout the *American Empower* Student's Book, learners are offered a wide variety of practice activities, plenty of controlled practice, and frequent opportunities for communicative spoken practice.

Results
Meaningful practice makes new language more memorable and leads to more efficient progress in language acquisition.

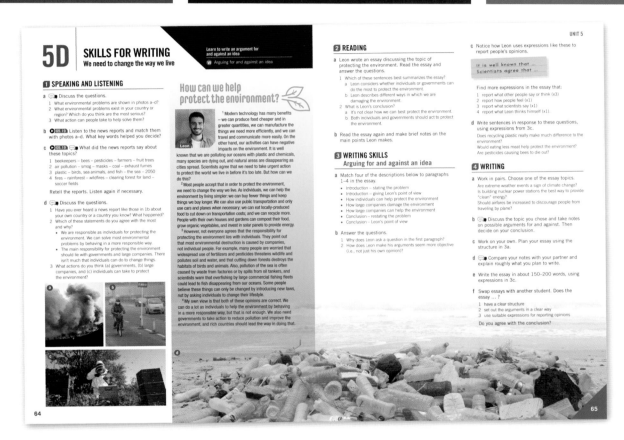

2 Beyond the classroom

There are plenty of opportunities for personalization.

Elena Pro, Teacher, EOI de San Fernando de Henares, Spain

Insights
Progress with language learning often requires work outside of the classroom, and different teaching models require different approaches.

Content
American Empower is available with a print workbook, online practice, documentary-style videos that expose learners to real-world English, plus additional resources with extra ideas and fun activities.

Results
This choice of additional resources helps teachers to find the most effective ways to motivate their students both inside and outside the classroom.

Unit overview

Unit Opener

Getting started page – Clear learning objectives to give an immediate sense of purpose.

↓

Lessons A and B

Grammar and Vocabulary – Input and practice of core grammar and vocabulary, plus a mix of skills.

— **Digital Workbook (online, mobile):** Grammar and Vocabulary

↓

Lesson C

Everyday English – Functional language in common, everyday situations.

— **Digital Workbook (online, mobile):** Listening and Speaking

↓

Unit Progress Test

↓

Lesson D

Integrated Skills – Practice of all four skills, with a special emphasis on writing.

— **Digital Workbook (online, mobile):** Reading and Writing

↓

Review

Extra practice of grammar, vocabulary, and pronunciation. Also a "Review your progress" section for students to reflect on the unit.

↓

Mid- / End-of-course test

↓

Additional practice

Further practice is available for outside of the class with these components.

Digital Workbook (online, mobile)

Workbook (printed)

Components

Resources – Available on cambridgeone.org

- Audio
- Video
- Unit Progress Tests (Print)
- Unit Progress Tests (Online)

- Mid- and end-of-course assessment (Print)
- Mid- and end-of-course assessment (Online)

- Digital Workbook (Online)
- Photocopiable Grammar, Vocabulary, and Pronunciation worksheets

4

Contents

Phonemic symbols and Irregular verbs p.164

5

This page is intentionally left blank.

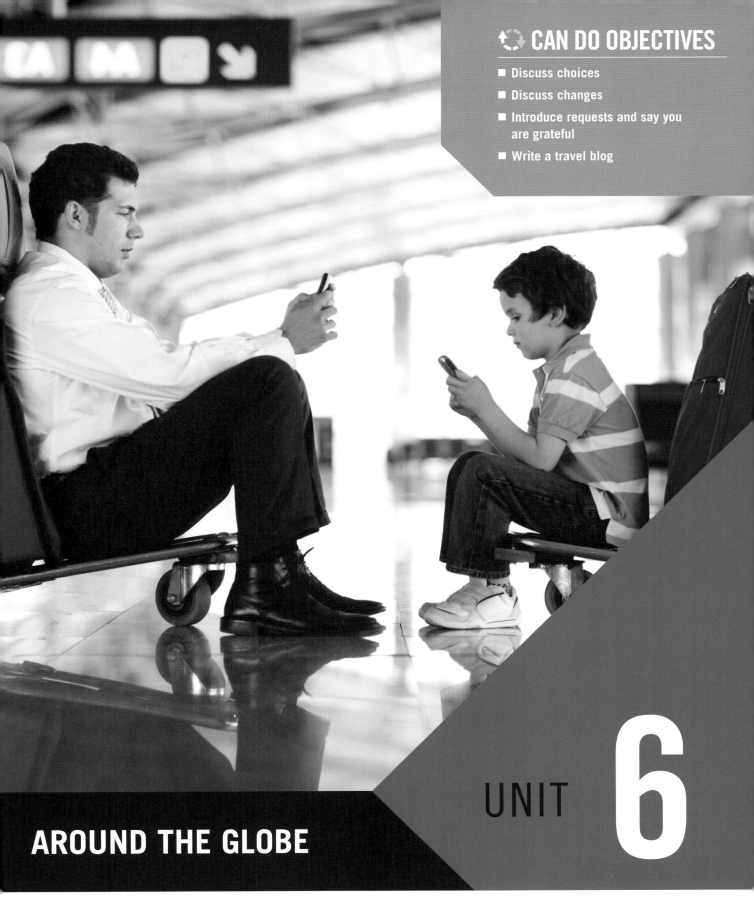

↻ CAN DO OBJECTIVES

- Discuss choices
- Discuss changes
- Introduce requests and say you are grateful
- Write a travel blog

UNIT 6

AROUND THE GLOBE

GETTING STARTED

a 💬🔊 Talk about the picture. What do you think about it?

1 Where are the man and the boy?
2 Why aren't they talking to each other?
3 What's on the man's phone? What's on the boy's phone?

b 💬🔊 Discuss the questions.

1 Do you prefer traveling alone or with other people? Why?
2 What do you usually do while you're waiting in an airport or a train/bus station?
3 What are the positives and negatives of going on long trips?

6A I'M NOT GOING TO TRY TO SEE EVERYTHING

Learn to discuss choices

G Gerunds and infinitives
V Travel and tourism

1 READING AND LISTENING

a Look at photos a–d and read about the four tourist attractions. Have you visited any of these places? Which one would you most like to visit?

b Read the tourist comments. Which are positive and which are negative?

1 " To see all these amazing things in gold and silver with precious stones like diamonds, and to know they've been used by kings and queens – it was wonderful! "

2 " It was too modern for me. I mean, it was interesting to see an amazing building and setting, but I like buildings with more historical objects. "

3 " All these incredible, old religious objects – they were in glass cases and too far away. I wanted to get much closer than that. "

4 " I've never seen so many beautiful, old paintings in one place – it was extraordinary. "

5 " We spent hours enjoying the amazing shapes and materials of the building – I could have stayed longer. "

6 " We had to keep walking and couldn't stop and look at the crown. It felt like high-pressure tourism. "

7 " Absolutely fascinating – I learned so much about the Ottoman Empire. "

8 " Overcrowded – and everyone rushing to take a photo of just one famous painting – not a pleasant experience. "

c Match comments 1–8 with the tourist attractions in 1a.

d ▶06.01 Listen to two tourists, Dia and Bernie. Which places in 1a do they mention? Do they have the same idea about sightseeing tours?

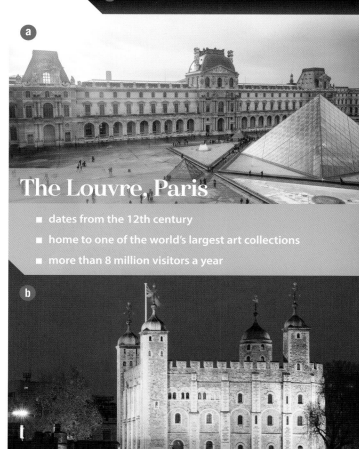

a

The Louvre, Paris

- dates from the 12th century
- home to one of the world's largest art collections
- more than 8 million visitors a year

b

The Tower of London

- dates from 1080
- home of the British Crown Jewels
- about 2.5 million visitors a year

e ▶06.01 Listen again and answer the questions.

Dia
1 Why did Dia join a tour?
2 What was her impression of the organization of the tour?
3 Where did she want to spend more time?
4 What did she and her friend do?

Bernie
1 How many people did Bernie travel with?
2 What was the problem with guidebooks and maps?
3 Why did they almost have an accident in Paris?
4 What was disappointing about the *Mona Lisa*?

f 💬 Discuss the questions.
1 Have you had experiences similar to Dia and Bernie?
2 How do you prefer to go sightseeing?
3 Dia and Bernie and some of the tourists in 1b mention some negative aspects of tourism. What others can you think of?
4 Do these negative aspects stop you from wanting to see traditional tourist sights? Why / Why not?

Bernie

Dia

Guggenheim Bilbao, Spain

- **designed by Canadian architect Frank Gehry and built in 1997**
- **modern museum made of titanium, glass, and limestone**
- **over 1 million visitors a year**

Topkapi Palace, Istanbul

- **main residence of Ottoman Sultans from 1465 to 1856**
- **contains holy relics from Muslim world**
- **about 3 million visitors a year**

2 GRAMMAR Gerunds and infinitives

a ▶ 06.02 Underline the correct verbs. Listen and check.

1 … it would be easy *to meet / meeting* people …
2 … we took off together *travel / to travel* around Europe.
3 *Drive / Driving* in Paris was really hard work …
4 Before *going / go* to the next place, I decided to *leave / leaving* the tour.

b Match rules a–d to sentences 1–4 in 2a.

a We use gerunds after prepositions.
b We use gerunds when it is the subject of a sentence.
c We use infinitives after adjectives.
d We use infinitives to talk about the purpose or reason for something.

c Match the verbs in **bold** with meaning a or b in each pair of sentences.

1 … the people organizing these tours **try** to include too much in the schedule.
2 I might **try** going on a tour of some kind.
  a do something to see what effect it has
  b attempt to do something (often unsuccessfully)

3 I **remember** visiting the incredible Guggenheim Museum …
4 … **remember** to be back at 10:30.
  a have a memory of doing something
  b not forget to do something

d Where do the objects (in parentheses) go in these sentences?

We could hear right behind us. (the bulls)
I noticed waving their arms at us. (all these people)

We can also use this pattern with *see, watch, observe, listen to, feel, smell.* What kinds of verbs are they?

e ≫ Now go to Grammar Focus 6A on p. 144.

f Complete the sentences with the correct form of the verbs in parentheses.

1 _____ (see) the pyramids for the first time was a magical experience.
2 You can't leave London without _____ (visit) the British Museum.
3 Why aren't you _____ (speak) to him in Spanish? He obviously can't understand you.
4 It's not possible _____ (go) to the museum in the evening. It closes at 5:00 p.m.
5 When you visit the Hermitage, remember _____ (look for) the two paintings by Leonardo da Vinci.
6 The guide was _____ (have) an argument with another tourist.
7 _____ (discover) Topkapi Palace in Istanbul was the highlight of my trip.
8 We went to Rome _____ (visit) the Colosseum and Roman Forum, but we found the baroque architecture just as interesting.
9 It was a small restaurant and I could smell our dinner _____ (be) cooked – delicious!
10 I remember _____ (see) the Sagrada Família for the first time – it was so original.

g 💬 Discuss the questions.

1 Why do you think we all like visiting the same tourist attractions?
2 Do you think it's important to see all the famous sights and landmarks if you visit a new place?
3 How do you think tourism will change in the future?

3 READING

a Read the comments from a tourism website about three destinations. Answer the questions.

1 What countries are the tourist destinations in?
2 Are the places well known?
3 Is the main tourist attraction in each place part of nature or is it man-made?

b Read the texts again. Are the sentences true or false?

1 Uruapan is an ancient city.
2 The Parícutin volcano is still active.
3 Colin and his girlfriend left Hanoi because of bad food.
4 The people of Ha Long Bay don't live on the islands.
5 The wooden constructions on Kizhi Island were built in the 1950s.
6 Emmy and her friends felt that visiting Kizhi Island was a special experience.

c 💬 Which place do you think sounds the most interesting? Which place sounds the least interesting? Why?

4 VOCABULARY
Travel and tourism

a Look at the adjectives in **bold** in the text. Do they have a positive or negative meaning?

b Answer the questions about the adjectives.

1 If something is *remarkable*, is there something special about it or is it pretty normal?
2 If you see something *memorable*, is it something that stays in your mind for a long time or do you forget it easily?
3 If you think something's *exotic*, does it seem foreign and unpleasant or foreign and interesting to you?
4 If a landmark is *breathtaking*, is it exciting and surprising or really high up?
5 If you feel that something's *impressive*, is it something you admire or just something that's very big?
6 If something's *unique*, how many are there of them in the world?
7 If you think something's *superb*, do you believe it's very spicy or of very high quality?
8 If you see something *astonishing*, are you very bored or very surprised?
9 If something's *stunning*, does it feel almost as though you've been hit by its beauty, or does it mean you think it's very old-fashioned?
10 If you think scenery is *dramatic*, is it pleasant and interesting or beautiful and exciting?

WHERE TO GO?

Have you planned your next vacation? Tell us about your favorite places and send us a photo.

URUAPAN

People always seem to go to the same places. I live in Mexico and tourists always visit places like Mexico City and Cancún. Not many tourists come to my hometown, Uruapan. It's one of the oldest cities in Mexico. A beautiful river – it's called "The river that sings" – runs through it, and there are spectacular waterfalls on the outskirts of the city. However, the most amazing feature you can see here is the nearby volcano, Parícutin. It really is **impressive**. You can go trekking up the volcano (it's about 420 meters high). The volcano is extinct, so it's perfectly safe. So for some history and some really **remarkable** scenery, Uruapan is a good choice. *Teresa*

HA LONG BAY

Last year, my girlfriend and I went to Vietnam for the first time. We loved it – the people were great and the food was **superb**. Hanoi is a busy city, but there are more **exotic** places you can escape to in Vietnam. The place we loved the most was Ha Long Bay where everyone lives in a floating house! On top of that, all around the bay there are **astonishing** islands made of limestone. Some of them look like beautiful towers – they're really **breathtaking**. And there are lakes and caves on some of the islands, as well as some very mischievous monkeys. Ha Long Bay is **dramatic** and beautiful. Many tourists have already discovered it – but it's still worth a visit. *Colin*

KIZHI ISLAND

If you want to see something original and **unique**, you should go to Kizhi Island in Russia. The whole island is like a museum of **stunning** wooden structures that look like they're right out of a fairy tale. The island's in the middle of Lake Onega in Karelia, Russia. In the 1950s, a lot of historic wooden buildings were moved from different parts of Karelia to the island in order to preserve them. A couple of years ago, a group of us went to St. Petersburg first, then on to Kizhi Island. It's the most **memorable** vacation I've ever had, and I felt like I'd been transported to another world. Although it's a UNESCO site, not too many people know about it, so you won't meet a lot of tourists. *Emmy*

c ▶ 06.07 **Pronunciation** Look at these adjectives from the text and mark the stress. Then listen and check.

impressive	stunning	breathtaking
remarkable	dramatic	memorable
superb	exotic	
astonishing	unique	

d 💬 Think of some interesting and beautiful things you've seen as a tourist. Choose adjectives from 4c to describe them. Then tell each other about the things you've seen.

e ≫ Now go to Vocabulary Focus 6A on p. 159.

5 READING AND SPEAKING

a ≫ **Communication 6A** Student A: Go to p. 133. Student B: Go to p. 132.

b Tell the class what you decided.

6B ABOUT HALF THE WORLD'S LANGUAGES WILL DISAPPEAR

Learn to discuss changes

G The passive
V Describing change

1 READING AND LISTENING

a 💬🔊 Work in small groups. Do the quiz together.

b ▶06.11 Listen to the first part of an interview with a language expert and check your answers. Then answer these questions.
1 What languages are most in danger of disappearing?
2 What is a "language hotspot?"

How much do you know about ... ?

LANGUAGES of the WORLD

Can you answer these questions?

1 How many independent countries are there in the world?
a) 120   **b)** nearly 200   **c)** nearly 500

2 How many spoken languages are there in the world?
a) around 500   **b)** around 3,000   **c)** around 7,000

3 Which one of these languages has over 400 million native speakers?
a) Portuguese   **b)** French   **c)** Spanish

4 What percentage of the world's population speaks Mandarin Chinese?
a) 4%   **b)** 14%   **c)** 24%

5 On average, how many languages die out every year?
a) 5   **b)** 25   **c)** 120

2 VOCABULARY Describing change

a Match the verbs in the box with the meanings.

| be lost   decline (x2)   decrease   deteriorate   die out |
| disappear   increase   preserve   revive |

1 keep as it is
2 stop existing (x3)
3 become more
4 become less or go down (x2)
5 bring back into existence
6 get worse (x2)

b Complete the sentences with the correct forms of the verbs in 2a and the information in 1b. More than one answer is possible.
1 The number of people who speak English is _____.
2 The number of minority languages is _____.
3 Many languages are in danger of _____.
4 Educating children may help to _____ a language.

c ▶06.12 **Pronunciation** Listen to the verb and noun forms of these words. Are they pronounced differently?

verb: increase   decrease   decline
noun: increase   decrease   decline

d ▶06.13 Say the words in **bold** in sentences 1–4. Then listen and check.
1 There has been a steady **increase** in world literacy.
2 The number of different English dialects is slowly **decreasing**.
3 There has been a gradual **decline** in student numbers.
4 The number of bilingual children has **increased** over the last 50 years.

e What is the noun form of these verbs? Choose the correct ending in the box. What changes do you need to make?

| -al   -ance   -tion |

1 disappear   2 deteriorate   3 revive   4 preserve

f 💬🔊 Think of three things which have increased or decreased in your country recently. Then compare with a partner.

3 READING

a Read about three languages. In what ways are they similar? In what ways are they different?

DANGER!
DYING LANGUAGES

About half the world's languages are in danger of dying out, and many have already been lost, sometimes without any written record to show what they were like. We look at three languages: one dead, one dying, and one that is being brought back to life thanks to one woman's dream.

BO In 2010, the last speaker of Bo, an ancient tribal language, died in the Andaman Islands, off the coast of India, breaking a 65,000-year link to one of the world's oldest cultures. Boa Sr was the last native who was fluent in Bo, which had been spoken since pre-Neolithic times.

Though the language was being studied and recorded by researchers, Boa Sr spent the last years of her life as the only speaker of the language, so she was unable to converse with anyone in her mother tongue. The Bo songs and stories which the old woman told couldn't be understood even by members of related tribes.

Andaman Islands

N|U

Hannah Koper is one of the few remaining speakers of a southern African language called N|u (the vertical line represents a clicking sound made with the tongue). Now most young people have no interest in learning N|u, which they see as an "ugly language, just for old people." Although efforts are being made to save the language from dying out by recording stories and by giving language classes for children, it seems unlikely to survive as a spoken language for more than a few years.

Hannah remembers: "We all used to get together and speak the language. We gathered together, we discussed issues, we laughed together in N|u."

WAMPANOAG

When the first European settlers landed in North America in 1620, they were helped by a Native American tribe called the Wampanoag, who showed them how to plant corn. The language died out in the early 19th century, and there were no fluent speakers of Wampanoag for more than 150 years.

However, one night a young woman named Jessie Little Doe Baird dreamed that her ancestors spoke to her in the Wampanoag language. Inspired by this, she first studied the language herself and then started a program to revive the language, using old written records and books written in the language. She and her husband are raising their daughter entirely in Wampanoag, and every summer they organize a "language camp," which is attended by a group of about 50 young people and where only Wampanoag is spoken. This is the first time a language with no living speakers for many generations has been revived in a Native American community, and there's a good chance that it will be spoken more widely by future generations of Wampanoag.

b Read the text again and take notes about each language:

1 number of speakers
2 increasing or decreasing
3 other important facts.

c 💬 Imagine you could ask each of the three people mentioned in the text a question. What would you ask? What answer do you think they would give?

4 GRAMMAR The passive

a Complete sentences 1–8 with the passive forms of the verbs in a–h.

1 Many languages _____ lost.
2 Bo was a local language which _____ since pre-Neolithic times.
3 The language _____ by researchers.
4 Her songs and stories couldn't _____ even by members of related tribes.
5 N|u _____ now only _____ by a few people.
6 Efforts _____ to save the language from dying out.
7 They _____ by a Native American tribe called the Wampanoag.
8 There's a good chance that it _____ more widely by future generations.

a is spoken
b were helped
c have already been
d will be spoken
e are being made
f was being studied
g had been spoken
h be understood

b How do we form the passive?

a *be* + past participle
b *have* + past participle
c *be* + infinitive

c Find and <u>underline</u> other examples of the passive in the text. What tense are they?

d ≫ Now go to Grammar Focus 6B on p. 144.

e Rewrite the paragraph using the passive so that the subject remains "the N|u language."

> The N|u language is in serious danger because people only speak it in a few small villages. In the past, people spoke it in a large region of South Africa and Namibia. Linguists have now recorded it and they've written it down, and teachers who have learned the language themselves are teaching it to children in schools.

f 💬 Think about languages in your country and discuss the questions.

1 What languages are spoken? What about dialects? Is there one "official" language or more than one?
2 Which languages or dialects do you think are spoken more and which are spoken less? Why?
3 Do you think people should be encouraged to use their own language, dialect, or accent? Why / Why not?

5 LISTENING AND SPEAKING

a You are going to listen to the rest of the interview with Professor Barnett, who tries to preserve endangered languages. How do you think he will answer these questions?

1 Does it matter if small languages die out … ?
 • to the people who speak that language
 • to the wider world
2 Isn't it a good idea for everyone to learn a global language?
3 Is it possible to stop languages from dying out?

b ▶ 06.16 Listen and check your ideas.

c ▶ 06.16 Listen again. Check (✓) the points he makes.

1 ☐ No one feels happy about their language dying out.
2 ☐ Languages are just as important as buildings.
3 ☐ You can translate everything from one language to another.
4 ☐ You can learn a "big" language and still keep your own language.
5 ☐ It's not good for children to be bilingual.
6 ☐ Children are the key to keeping languages alive.
7 ☐ Technology can help keep languages from dying out.

d Which points in 5c do you agree with? Are there any you disagree with? Why?

e ≫ **Communication 6B** Work in two pairs. Pair A: Go to p. 130. Pair B: Go to p. 133.

f 💬 Work with a partner from the other pair. Have a discussion, using the arguments you prepared. Report back to the class which points you agree on.

6C EVERYDAY ENGLISH
Do you mind if I ask you a favor?

1 LISTENING

a 💬 Answer the questions.

1 When was the last time you had to ask a friend or a family member for a favor?
2 What kind of favor was it?
3 How do you feel about asking someone a favor?

b Look at the photo of Lena. What is she doing? What favor do you think she might ask her brother, José?

c ▶️ 06.17 Listen to Part 1. Were your ideas in 1b correct? What is the favor?

d ▶️ 06.17 Listen to Part 1 again. Answer the questions.

1 When do Lena and Maddie need help?
2 How does Lena feel about asking José?
3 How do Lena and Maddie feel after talking to José?

2 CONVERSATION SKILLS Introducing requests

a ▶️ 06.18 Read the conversation below and then listen to an excerpt from Part 1. What is the difference?

LENA	José?
JOSÉ	Yeah.
LENA	Can you help me and Maddie move this Friday?
JOSÉ	Sure.

b ▶️ 06.18 Lena and Maddie go through four steps to introduce the request. Put the steps in the correct order. Listen again and check.

1 They make the request.
2 They show that they realize they're asking a big favor.
3 They say they want to make a request.
4 They give a reason for needing to make the request.

c Why do Lena and Maddie introduce their request carefully? Choose the correct answer.

1 Lena doesn't know José very well.
2 Lena and José had an argument recently.
3 They realize they're asking José a big favor.
4 Lena is worried that José will get fired.

d Complete the beginnings in A with a word in the box. Then match A and B to make expressions that introduce requests.

---

like   if   mind   to   if

A
1 Do you mind _____
2 I'm really sorry _____
3 There's an idea I'd _____
4 I was wondering _____
5 I hope you don't _____

B
a ask you this, but …
b you wouldn't mind … ?
c I ask you something?
d my asking, but …
e to run past you.

e Answer the questions in 2d and use the replies below.

1 What do you say to the requests to encourage the speaker?
2 Which two replies can be used with requests 1, 4, and 5?
3 Which reply matches request 3?

> What is it?

> No, that's fine.

> No, not at all.

> Go right ahead.

3 USEFUL LANGUAGE
Showing you are grateful

a Maddie thanks José and then shows how grateful she is. Complete Maddie's sentence.

Thank you. That's _____ _____ of you.

▶ 06.19 Listen and check.

b Put the words in the correct order to make expressions.

1 really / it / appreciate / we
2 really / grateful / we're
3 it's / of / kind / you / so
4 don't / to / I / thank / know / you / how

c Look at these replies to the expressions in 3b. Which one is not suitable? Why?

1 Oh, don't worry about it.   4 I'm glad you're grateful.
2 I'm happy to help.   5 It's not a problem.
3 It's no trouble at all.   6 My pleasure.

4 LISTENING

a 💬▣ Look at the photo below and discuss the questions. Why do you think … ?

1 José is saying, "Great, thanks!"
2 Matt is saying, "No problem."

b ▶ 06.20 Listen to Part 2 and check your answers.

c ▶ 06.20 Listen again. Are the sentences true or false?

1 Matt invites José to a game.
2 José needs help with a move on Saturday.
3 There are games on Friday and Saturday.
4 Matt offers to rent a truck to help with the move.
5 José offers to buy tickets if they finish the move early.

5 PRONUNCIATION
Sound and spelling: Consonant sounds

a Notice the **bold** consonant sounds. Match the underlined sounds a–h with consonant sounds 1–8.

1 ☐ /θ/ **th**irty   5 ☐ /ʃ/ **sh**op
2 ☐ /ð/ **th**ey   6 ☐ /ʒ/ u**s**ually
3 ☐ /s/ **s**ay   7 ☐ /tʃ/ **ch**oose
4 ☐ /z/ **z**ero   8 ☐ /dʒ/ **j**eans

a I'm really <u>s</u>orry to ask you …
b My plea<u>s</u>ure …
c Do you <u>th</u>ink it'll be a problem?
d I need to <u>ch</u>eck with Sonia …
e I'm really into science fi<u>ct</u>ion.
f It's time you had a vacation toge<u>th</u>er.
g She likes taking photos of bri<u>dg</u>es.
h I could clo<u>s</u>e up on Friday.

▶ 06.21 Listen and check.

b Find a sound from 5a in the following words:

1 ideas   5 bother
2 earth   6 sugar
3 television   7 science
4 jewel   8 future

▶ 06.22 Listen and check. Then practice saying the words.

6 SPEAKING

a Think of a big favor to ask your partner. Think of a reason why you need to ask this favor.

b 💬▣ Take turns making your requests. Make sure you introduce your request carefully. If your partner agrees to your request, show that you're grateful.

Great, thanks.

No problem.

I hope you don't mind my asking.

No, not at all.

I know that you're usually really busy on weekends …

Well, this weekend looks OK at the moment.

✅ UNIT PROGRESS TEST

➡ CHECK YOUR PROGRESS

You can now do the Unit Progress Test.

6D | SKILLS FOR WRITING
The scenery was fantastic

1 SPEAKING AND LISTENING

a 💬🔊 Look at the photos of the top five tourist attractions in the U.S. What do you know about them? Why do you think people want to see them? Which place would you most like to visit? Why?

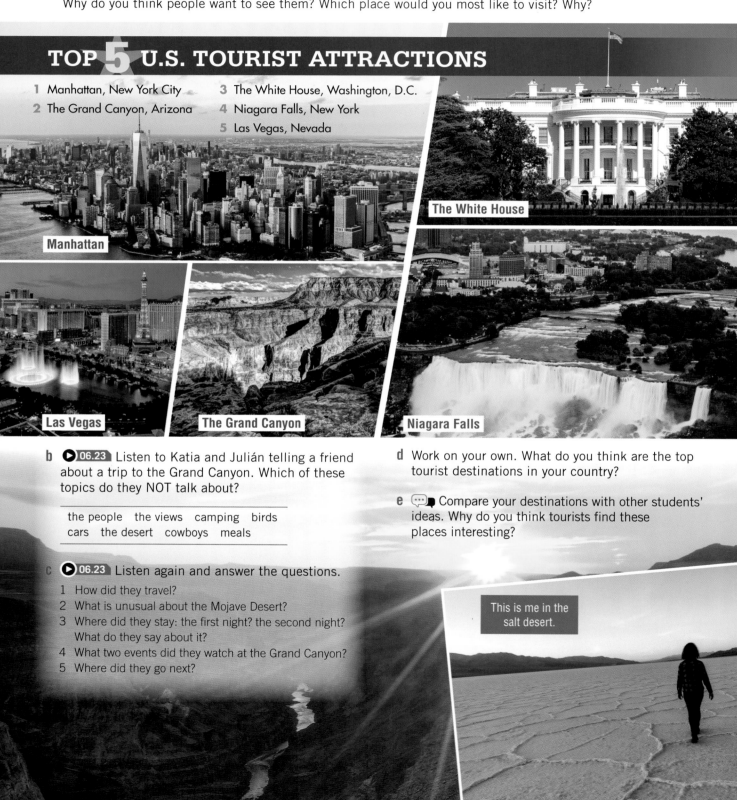

TOP 5 U.S. TOURIST ATTRACTIONS

1 Manhattan, New York City
2 The Grand Canyon, Arizona
3 The White House, Washington, D.C.
4 Niagara Falls, New York
5 Las Vegas, Nevada

The White House

Manhattan

Las Vegas

The Grand Canyon

Niagara Falls

b ▶️ 06.23 Listen to Katia and Julián telling a friend about a trip to the Grand Canyon. Which of these topics do they NOT talk about?

the people   the views   camping   birds
cars   the desert   cowboys   meals

c ▶️ 06.23 Listen again and answer the questions.
1 How did they travel?
2 What is unusual about the Mojave Desert?
3 Where did they stay: the first night? the second night? What do they say about it?
4 What two events did they watch at the Grand Canyon?
5 Where did they go next?

d Work on your own. What do you think are the top tourist destinations in your country?

e 💬🔊 Compare your destinations with other students' ideas. Why do you think tourists find these places interesting?

This is me in the salt desert.

2 READING

a Read Katia's travel blog about their trip. What information does it contain that was not in the recording?

Around the
GRAND CANYON

Driving to the Grand Canyon was an experience in itself. On the historic Route 66, we passed through the heart of the Mojave Desert, which is a huge, flat salt desert – it was the first time we had seen salt plains. We stopped off at a small town called Williams, where we saw cowboys and a re-enactment of an old shootout that had taken place there in the 1800s.

It was late when we finally found a restaurant, where they let us put up our tent behind the building. To our horror, the air mattress had a hole in it, so we had another uncomfortable night's sleep. I could feel stones pressing into my back all night! In the morning, we woke and drove the final 20 kilometers to the canyon. It was breathtaking ... it's hard to describe in words the grandeur and beauty of this natural phenomenon – it was the experience of a lifetime. We drove around the South Rim, which has superb views down into the canyon itself, until we found a campsite. Luckily, we found a spot even though it was peak season. We ate, then went to the Desert Watchtower to watch the sun going down – just amazing.

At 4:45 a.m., we woke up and took a walk to watch the sun rise, which was a whole new experience as the light and the shadows made everything look different. After breakfast, we headed up to the village where a bus took us to the other part of the South Rim. We took a short hike and we were very lucky to see a condor, as their numbers have declined and there are now less than 300 left in the wild – they are huge and very impressive. We watched it circling right above our heads. Again, the scenery was fantastic, and we saw the canyon from a few different viewpoints.

After that we drove to Lake Mead for a few days to relax before the madness of Las Vegas. Vegas – here we come!

Julián looking down into the canyon.

3 WRITING SKILLS
Using descriptive language

a Katia says the sunset was *amazing*. Find five other adjectives in the blog that mean *very beautiful* or *very big*.

b Look at the adjectives and phrases in the box. Which of them have a positive meaning and which have a negative meaning?

disappointing   fabulous   awesome
uninspiring   mind-blowing   ordinary
unbelievable   out of this world   dull
awe-inspiring   unforgettable

c Which adjectives/phrases in 3b can be used to complete these sentences?

1 Without a doubt, the scenery was absolutely
　　　　.
2 I don't know. The scenery was a little _____.

Can you think of adverbs to replace *absolutely* and *a little*?

d Change these sentences to make the meaning stronger. Use adjectives and phrases from 3a and 3b. More than one answer is possible.

1 Manhattan was good, and I thought the buildings were very nice.
2 Niagara Falls was beautiful. We went on a boat below the falls – it was very good.
3 People say that Las Vegas is a nice place to visit, but I thought it was not very good.

e Katia also uses three expressions with *experience* to describe the trip. Find the examples in 2a and complete 1–3.

1 It was an experience _____.
2 It was the experience _____.
3 ... which was a whole _____ experience.

f 💬 Think of a place you have visited. Write sentences about your experience using language in 3a–e. Then discuss it.

4 WRITING

a Choose one of the photos, or think of one of your own travel photos. Plan a travel blog around this photo. Take notes on:

- where you went
- what you did
- what you saw
- what it was like.

b Write the travel blog. Include language from 3a–e.

c 💬 Switch travel blogs with other students. Ask and answer questions. Do the descriptions make you want to visit the place? Why / Why not?

UNIT 6
Review and extension

1 GRAMMAR

a Correct the mistakes in these sentences.

1 Do you find it easy relax on the weekend?
2 What kinds of things do you do for help you relax?
3 Do you have a series of household tasks you need to remember doing?
4 In your neighborhood, do you notice people to do the same kinds of things as you do?
5 Do you remember to do the same kinds of things on the weekend when you were a child?

b 💬🎙 Ask each other the corrected questions.

c Put the verbs in parentheses in the correct passive or active form.

This small pot ¹_____ (give) to me by my great-grandfather about 10 years ago. It's Egyptian. He ²_____ (buy) it about 60 years ago. Apparently it ³_____ (discover) in the desert by an Egyptian farmer. Then it ⁴_____ (see) by a soldier during the war. He ⁵_____ (pass) through a village where the pot ⁶_____ (clean). My great-grandfather ⁷_____ (say) the pot ⁸_____ (sell) to the soldier for the price of a cup of coffee. He ⁹_____ (pay) about $30 for it after the war. It ¹⁰_____ (value) recently by an expert, and it's now worth more than $2,000.

2 VOCABULARY

a Write the correct adjectives in the blanks.

1 We had a fantastic meal followed by an incredible concert. It really was a m_____ evening.
2 They have a really i_____ collection of old movie posters – I've never seen so many.
3 I come from Tahiti so for me, somewhere like Canada is e_____.
4 She paid a lot of money for her new evening dress. But it was worth it – she looks s_____ in it.
5 My favorite act in the circus was the high-wire acrobats. They were so skilled – their performance was b_____.

b Choose the correct word in *italics*.

Robinson's used to be my favorite department store. However, in the past few years, I've noticed there's been a ¹*decreasing / deterioration* in service. Years ago, the owners used to walk around the store and chat with customers, but not anymore. I wish they'd ²*revive / increase* that and ³*preservation / preserve* those old traditions with a personal touch. However, the Robinson family have all ⁴*died out / been lost* now, and the store's owned by some anonymous company. They've ⁵*declined / decreased* the number of store assistants who can help you. Instead there's been an ⁶*increased / increase* in self-service check-outs and face-to-face contact has ⁷*been lost / revived*. I think it's a shame.

3 WORDPOWER *out*

a ▶06.24 Listen to the short conversations. What multi-word verb with *out* is used to replace the underlined words?

1 Yes, if I keep working 14-hour days, I'll <u>become exhausted</u>. _____ out
2 I feel like I'm going to <u>faint</u>. _____ out
3 I just need to <u>calculate</u> the total cost. _____ out
4 I've <u>argued</u> with my brother and we're not speaking. _____ out
5 Yes, but didn't we <u>finish the</u> milk? _____ out
6 But of all the applicants, Maria really <u>is noticeably better</u>. _____ out
7 But he's <u>become</u> a very nice young man. _____ out
8 I'm going to lie by the swimming pool with a cold drink and just <u>relax</u>. _____ out

b Write multi-word verbs with *out* in the blanks. Think carefully about the correct verb form to use.

1 The weather was terrible this morning, but it's _____ to be a beautiful day.
2 His way of _____ is to play video games and forget daily life.
3 She was getting annoyed with the bad behavior of the class, and her patience was beginning to _____.
4 All the staff are saying that they're going to _____ if they keep working so hard.
5 This model really _____ as being more economical than all other cars of this size.
6 I'm trying to _____ how much tax I have to pay, but it's really hard.
7 The sight of blood makes him _____.
8 He always _____ with his friends – he's very difficult to get along with.

c Take notes about the following questions.

1 Have you ever fallen out with another family member? Why?
2 What do you like to do to chill out?
3 Have you ever passed out? If so, how did it happen?
4 Who's a famous person that you think really stands out? Why do you think so?
5 What kinds of jobs do you think could result in burn out?

d 💬🎙 Discuss your answers to the questions.

⟳ REVIEW YOUR PROGRESS

How well did you do in this unit? Write 3, 2, or 1 for each objective.
3 = very well   2 = well   1 = not so well

I CAN ...	
discuss choices	☐
discuss changes	☐
introduce requests and say I am grateful	☐
write a travel blog.	☐

↺ **CAN DO OBJECTIVES**

- Discuss living in cities
- Discuss changes to a home
- Imagine how things could be
- Write an email to complain

UNIT **7**

CITY LIVING

GETTING STARTED

a 💬 Look at the picture and answer the questions.

1 Look at the buildings. Which one is new, or modern? How is it different from the older building beside it? How is it similar?

2 What do you think of the modern building? Do you think it is … ?
interesting   outrageous   ridiculous   amusing
ugly   harmonious

3 What do you think the architect of the modern building was aiming to achieve? How successful was he/she?

b 💬 Discuss the questions.

1 Think of modern buildings that you know. What do you like / not like about them?

2 Do you think new buildings should fit in with their surroundings or stand out from them? Why?

3 Do you think it's right to develop and alter city neighborhoods or should they be preserved?

1 SPEAKING

a 💬 What kind of stress is caused by crowds? How do you think the people in the two photos feel?

b 💬 Imagine a third photo of city life. What might it show? Discuss your ideas.

2 READING

a The article below is from an online group called the Slow Movement. Read the title. What do you think the group believes?

1 Success isn't as important as people think.
2 You shouldn't let work take over your life.
3 Modern life is bad for our health.

Quick – Slow Down!

Speed Worship

We love speed. When it comes to doing business and connecting with people, speed is important. We need to get our work done faster. We worry that we're too slow, that we aren't efficient enough or productive enough to succeed. We need to get there first. How do we do this? We speed up. Why? Because we seem to associate "slow" with failure, inefficiency, and even worse: laziness.

City Life

Many people complain that they don't have enough time. They have too much work to do every day, and there are always too many things that they haven't done. There is pressure to be available 24/7 – to colleagues, clients, and friends. We spend around 13 hours a week on emails and an average of three hours a day on social networking sites. City living can make things worse – we spend 106 days of our life looking for a parking space and up to three days a year in traffic jams. We have less time to relax, and this makes us more impatient and less polite. Even birds are affected by the pace of urban living – blackbirds in cities get up earlier and go to sleep later than rural blackbirds.

Time Poverty and Sleep Debt

Economist Juliet Schor calculated that people in most jobs now work the equivalent of a full month more each year than they did two decades earlier. In addition to this, scientist Russell Foster says that people get about two hours less sleep than they did 60 years ago.

This results in "sleep debt." In other words, people have so little sleep over such a long period of time that they are permanently tired. Studies done on doctors who didn't get enough sleep showed that they had the same reaction speed as people who had drunk two glasses of beer. Being so tired can also seriously affect your health – scientists have discovered a link between sleep debt and cancer, heart disease, diabetes, infections, and obesity.

Slow Seeing

We are in such a hurry that we are creating big problems for ourselves. The answer to this is

b Read "Quick – Slow Down!" quickly and check your ideas from 2A.

c Read the article again. What connection does the writer make between … ?

1 speed and business
2 slowness and laziness
3 time and city life
4 relaxing and our mood
5 work and sleep
6 "sleep debt" and alcohol
7 tiredness and health

d 💬🔊 How could you live more slowly? Compare your ideas.

Rules For Slowing Down

1 Put your feet up and stare idly out the window. (Warning: Do not attempt this while driving.)

2 Think about things; take your time. Do not be pushed into answering questions. A response is not the same as an answer.

3 Yawn often. Medical studies have shown that yawning may be good for you.

4 Bright lights and screens before bed will make sleeping difficult. So avoid gaming and social networking late in the evening.

5 Spend more time in bed. When it's time to get out of bed in the morning, don't. Sit there for half an hour and do nothing. Then get up slowly.

6 Read long, slow stories.

7 Spend more time in the bath.

8 Practice doing nothing. (Yes, this is the difficult one.)

simple: slow down! Slowing down gives us the opportunity to see things more clearly and make the right decisions, and in the end it may help us to have better ideas and a healthier life. Einstein, one of the greatest scientific minds of all time, spent a lot of time daydreaming, and psychologists agree that this helps us to be more creative. So sit back and do nothing for a little while – your brain and body will thank you for it.

e Read "Rules for Slowing Down!" Are they the same as your ideas in 2d? Which ones are … ?

- things you do already
- things you don't do, but you think are a good idea
- things you think are a bad idea

3 GRAMMAR *too / enough; so / such*

a Put *too*, *too much*, *too many*, or *enough* in the correct place in each sentence. Then check your answers in the article "Quick – Slow Down!"

1 We worry that we're slow.
2 We aren't efficient or productive to succeed.
3 Many people complain that they don't have time.
4 They have work to do every day.
5 There are always things that they haven't done.

b Look at the sentences in 3a again. Did you put the words before or after … ?

1 an adjective   2 a noun

c Complete the rules with the words in the box.

> an adjective   count   after
> a noun   before   noncount

1 We use *too* before _____, but *too much* or *too many* before _____.
2 We use *too much* before _____ nouns and *too many* before _____ nouns.
3 *Enough* always comes _____ an adjective but _____ a noun.

d Complete the sentences with *so* or *such*.

1 People get _____ little sleep over _____ a long period of time that they are permanently tired.
2 Being _____ tired can also seriously affect your health.
3 We are in _____ a hurry that we are creating big problems for ourselves.

e ≫ Now go to Grammar Focus 7A on p. 146.

f Find and correct the mistake in each sentence.

1 I have such much work to do that I often have to work on weekends.
2 You spend too many time in front of the computer.
3 We don't have money enough to buy a new car.
4 He doesn't like his job, but he's too much lazy to look for a better one.
5 Cheer up! Why are you always in so a bad mood?
6 I'll have to draw the plan again. It isn't enough clear.

g Write four sentences about your everyday life and work/studies. They can be true or false. Include *too*, *enough*, *so*, or *such*.

I have so many clothes that I never know what to wear.

h Work in groups. Read your sentences from 3g. Can your group guess which sentences are true and which are false?

4 READING AND LISTENING

a Look at the cities in photos a–d. What do you think the term "smart city" means?

b ▶07.05 Listen to the interview. What are the two main ideas of a "smart city?" Choose two of the answers below.

1 People in it have a good quality of life.
2 It responds to people's needs.
3 It encourages people to have new ideas.

c ▶07.05 Listen again. What new information do you hear about … ?

1 traffic in London, U.K.
2 smog and bicycles in Mexico City
3 energy use in Masdar, U.A.E.
4 life in Songdo, South Korea

5 VOCABULARY
Describing life in cities

a Match 1–7 and a–g to make collocations.

1 ☐ local	a development
2 ☐ traffic	b pollution
3 ☐ quality	c transportation
4 ☐ urban	d of life
5 ☐ public	e congestion
6 ☐ air	f space
7 ☐ parking	g residents

b Find collocations in **a** that mean:

1 the level of enjoyment and health in someone's life
2 the people in a particular area
3 the problem of too many vehicles in the streets
4 a place to leave your car
5 the process in which a city grows or changes
6 buses, trains, subways, etc.
7 damage caused to the air by harmful substances.

c Use two or three of the collocations in sentences about the place where you are now.

d 💬 Read your sentences aloud. Do other students agree?

SMART CITIES:
Are these the cities of the future?

In London, U.K., cars pay to enter the city center, and you only need a single card for the whole public transportation system.

Songdo, a new city in South Korea, was built with 40% green spaces throughout and public transportation options like water taxis to cut down on air pollution.

Masdar, U.A.E., is built in the desert, and solar panels provide all its energy needs.

Mexico City has a smog-eating building and fewer parking spaces to encourage p[ublic] transportation and bicycling – that's why [the] city has over 6,000 public bikes.

6 LISTENING

a ▶07.06 Listen to Daniela and Richard talking about the cities they live in. Answer the questions.

1 Do they like living there? Why / Why not?
2 Do they think it fits the idea of a "smart city?"

b ▶07.06 Which of these points do Daniela and Richard make? Listen again to check.

Daniela

1 Bogotá has a rapid bus system and discourages driving.
2 The center of Bogotá is closed off to traffic every Sunday.
3 Bogotá has no problems with traffic or air pollution.

Richard

4 Bangkok is disorganized but full of life.
5 It's easy to find places to sit and relax in the city center.
6 The center of Bangkok is too expensive for ordinary people to live there.

7 SPEAKING

a Think about the town you're in now. In what ways does it fit the idea of a "smart city"? What are the good and bad points about living there? Take notes.

b 💬 Discuss your ideas, using the expressions in 5b. Does everybody agree?

1 READING

a 💬 Discuss the questions.

1 What kinds of reality TV shows are there in your country?
2 Do you enjoy these shows? Why / Why not?

b ≫ **Communication 7B** Now go to p. 131.

c 💬 Look at the photo from the article and answer the questions.

- Where is the woman?
- Why do you think she's there?
- What do you think she's doing?

d Read the article quickly. What is the main point the critic wants to make about reality TV? Choose the correct answer.

1 We no longer need stories for entertainment. Real people are more interesting.
2 Reality TV is in danger of creating unreal expectations about life.
3 A lot of the "reality" in reality TV shows is invented.

e Read the article again. In what way does the writer think reality is managed in these kinds of TV shows?

- survival
- cooking
- home renovation
- garden makeover

f 💬 If what the writer says is true, … ?

- does this make the shows less enjoyable
- are TV producers and directors being dishonest

WHO PUTS THE "REAL" IN REALITY TV?

These days we like our entertainment to be real. We watch people go to extreme environments to see who's the most successful survivor. We can't get enough of chefs fighting it out to prove they're the best. Then there are the people who transform their homes, their gardens, or even themselves in front of a TV camera. But what's really going on in these shows?

Let's imagine someone named Julie. She isn't a real person – I made her up – but she could be real. She's the kind of person who might appear on a reality TV show. You know, she's someone who lives a quiet life in a small town somewhere, but then she decides to do something really extreme and dangerous on TV. Of course, it helps that she has one or two big fears hiding under that quiet exterior – the type of thing that's going to come to the surface when, like the woman in the picture above, she's struggling to escape or survive … but, of course, we tend to forget the crew that's filming all this. I'm sure they're very helpful. It's also possible that the director asked Julie to crawl through the mud more than once – just to get a better shot.

What about those cooking shows? They're all good cooks, aren't they? Well, yes, they are. But that's not always why they get chosen. TV producers want drama, so they need a range of personalities on the show. Imagine a cooking competition where the cooks all got along really well and cooperated. In other words, no conflict. Is that the kind of reality we want to watch on TV?

A NEW LIFE IN 5 MINUTES

And then there's the makeover show – you know, the new home, the new garden, or the new-look you. Haven't you ever stopped to wonder how people on these shows miraculously have a new kitchen after just one weekend? Remember your family's kitchen renovations? They took forever. On these shows, they like to speed up reality a little. While many of these shows use professional tradespeople, others claim the renovation is all the work of the contestants. But did Julie really manage to repaint those walls between breakfast and lunch by herself? No, the director had some of it done by a professional painter. It probably would have taken Julie all weekend.

And wasn't Julie clever coming up with such a beautiful design for her garden? It's so good you would almost think that a landscape architect had done it. The chances are that's exactly what happened – the TV company got the design done by an expert.

DISASTER STRIKES … OR DOES IT?

Finally, let's not forget those little crisis moments along the way. Julie would love to be able to buy that designer fridge because it would make all the difference to her home makeover. But no, she only has so much to spend and this just might blow her budget. Don't panic, dear viewer, the TV production company has a lot of money, and there's nothing to stop them from increasing Julie's budget. The production company can afford to let Julie buy ten designer fridges without stopping to think about it.

TV production companies would like us to believe that what we see on TV actually happens. Well, it does, but only sort of. What we're really seeing is a kind of managed reality. Real reality on TV would probably be like real life – a little slow and boring.

2 VOCABULARY Movies and TV

a Look at the highlighted words in "Who Puts the 'Real' in Reality TV?" With a TV show, who ... ?

1 organize(s) everything
2 tell(s) the actors what to do
3 work(s) as a technical team
4 watch(es) the show

b Match the words in **bold** in 1–4 to definitions a–d.

1 ☐ There are only eight characters in the movie – that means a small **cast**.
2 ☐ It's a very well-written movie with a great **script** – there are some very funny scenes.
3 ☐ I loved everything about the movie except for the **soundtrack** – too much jazz for my taste.
4 ☐ The movie opens with a long **shot** of the main character walking along the edge of a cliff.

a the sounds and music
b a sequence of film from a camera
c the story the actors act out
d all the actors in a production

c ⫸ Now go to Vocabulary Focus 7B on p. 160.

3 GRAMMAR Causative *have / get*

a Look at the examples from "Who Puts the 'Real' in Reality TV?" What is the meaning of *have* and *get*? Choose the correct answer.

The director ***had*** *some of it* done by a professional painter.
The TV company ***got*** *the design* done by an expert.
1 someone arranges for another person to do something
2 someone has done something later than planned

b ⫸ Now go to Grammar Focus 7B on p. 146.

c 💬 Discuss these topics. What things do you do yourself? What things do you have/get done?

personal appearance   household jobs   vehicles you own

I have my hair cut once a month.

My father has his car serviced twice a year.

I always decorate the house myself.

4 VOCABULARY Houses

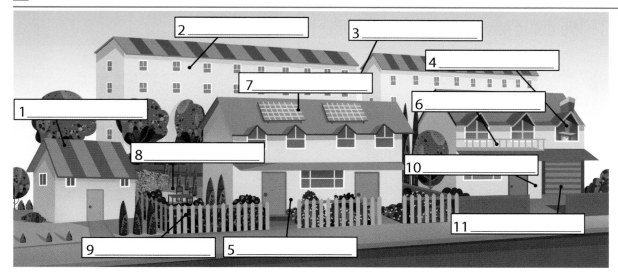

1 _____
2 _____
3 _____
4 _____
5 _____
6 _____
7 _____
8 _____
9 _____
10 _____
11 _____

a Use the words to label the parts of the picture.

cottage   garden   alley   fireplace   fence   garage   balcony   single-family home
multiple-family dwelling   apartment building   solar panels

b 💬 Discuss the questions.

1 Does the house or apartment you live in have solar panels? Does anyone in your neighborhood use a different source of electricity?
2 Why do people have gardens?
3 How do you keep your home warm or cool? Do you have a fireplace and/or air conditioner?
4 Do you prefer fences or walls around gardens?
5 What kind of housing is most common where you live: single-family, multiple-family, cottages, or apartment buildings?
6 Do you have a balcony? What can you do with a balcony?
7 Where can you find alleys? Are they common where you live?

5 LISTENING

Antonia

a 💬 In your area, if people want to do renovations to their home, do they do it themselves or do they usually have them done by an expert?

b ▶ 07.10 Listen to Antonia and Rob talk about house renovations. Do they feel the same about renovating?

c ▶ 07.10 Check (✓) what Antonia and Rob have done. Then listen and check your answers.

Antonia
☐ pulled out the original kitchen cabinet
☐ updated the bathroom
☐ uncovered the original fireplace
☐ repainted the kitchen
☐ painted the bedroom

Rob
☐ knocked down a wall
☐ bought all the supplies he needs
☐ hired a professional to help him
☐ took his kids to sports practice
☐ discovered a place to make a playroom

d 💬 Do you know people like Antonia and Rob? What do you think about them?

6 SPEAKING

Rob

a 💬 Imagine you are a TV producer for a new home renovation show. Rob's wife has contacted the show to ask for help with their renovation. Think about:

• what makes your show interesting to watch (e.g., time and budget limits)
• what you could do with Rob's new space
• what you will get Rob / professional workers to do.

b Present your ideas to the rest of the class. Decide which ideas would make the most interesting show.

7C EVERYDAY ENGLISH
We could have a table or something here

Learn to imagine how things could be
P Stress in compound nouns
S Using vague language

1 LISTENING

a Look at the photo. What type of person would work at a furniture store like this one?

b ▶ 07.11 Listen to Part 1. Were your ideas correct?

c ▶ 07.11 Listen again and take notes on the topics below.

1 What Tanya is good at doing
2 What Tanya likes about her job
3 Brian's old job
4 Why Brian has to leave

2 PRONUNCIATION
Stress in compound nouns

a ▶ 07.12 Listen to the compound words and answer the questions.

A	B
bookshelf	love seat
lampshade	living room

1 Which part of the word has the main stress in group A and group B? The first or the second?
2 Look at the first part of the compound words. Are they nouns or adjectives?

b Complete the rules.

> If a compound noun is noun + noun, we usually stress the _____ word.
> If a compound noun is adjective + noun, we usually stress the _____ word.

c ▶ 07.13 <u>Underline</u> the stressed part of these compound words. Then listen and check. Try saying them with the correct stress.

flower garden
front yard
nightclub
cell phone
throw pillow

3 SPEAKING AND LISTENING

a 💬 Think about where you live and answer the questions.

1 Is it easy to find an apartment or room to rent? Why / Why not?
2 Do you think it is better to own a place or to rent one? Why?
3 What kind place do you live in? What kind would you like to live in?

b ▶ 07.14 Listen to Part 2. Which sentence describes what happens?

1 The real estate agent is enthusiastic and Brian and Arun like things about the apartment.
2 Brian and Arun like the apartment, but they think it's too small and the agent agrees with them.
3 The agent is enthusiastic about the apartment, but Brian and Arun think it won't work for them.

c How does the real estate agent describe the apartment? Choose words or phrases for each room.

cozy   a nice view   quiet   practical
smaller   perfect   convenient

1 the living room   2 the second bedroom   3 the kitchen

d According to Brian and Arun, what problems does the apartment have?

e ▶ 07.15 Listen to Part 3. How is this apartment different from the one in Part 2? Do Brian and Arun get the apartment?

f ▶ 07.15 Are the sentences true or false? Listen again and check.

1 The apartment has been on the market for a few weeks.
2 Brian is worried it's too expensive for them.
3 Brian and Arun start thinking about how to arrange the apartment.
4 No one else has expressed interest in the apartment.
5 Brian and Arun need time to decide what to do.

4 USEFUL LANGUAGE Imagining how things could be

a ▶ **07.15** In Part 3, Brian and Arun imagine how the apartment might look if they lived in it. Complete these sentences from the conversation. Use modal verbs and main verbs. Then listen and check.

1 Look, this ____ ____ a separate living area by the window.
2 We ____ ____ some plants and some bookshelves there …
3 And this ____ ____ a great dining area.
4 I ____ ____ a big TV right here.

b What does sentence 3 in 4a mean?

1 We'd need to do some work on it.
2 It could have this function.
3 It's a dining room.

c 💬 Work in small groups. Look at your classroom and try to imagine it as one of the following:

- an office   - a library   - a small apartment.

Imagine how it might look and what might be in it. Use expressions in 4a.

d 💬 Present your ideas to other groups. Who had the most interesting ideas?

5 CONVERSATION SKILLS Using vague language

a ▶ **07.16** Listen to the conversation. Where do the speakers add the phrases in parentheses?

1 This could be a separate living area by the window. (kind of)
2 We could have plants and bookshelves there, or a big lamp. (and things)
3 We could have a table here, and some cool lights. (or something)

b The phrases in 5a are examples of vague language. Why do the speakers use vague language?

- because they're not sure how the apartment should look
- because they're in a hurry and can't think of the exact words

c **Pronunciation** Is the vague language stressed or unstressed? What do you notice about the pronunciation of *and*, *of*, and *or* in the phrases?

d Look at these vague phrases. Which phrases in 5a could they replace?

1 and things like that
2 sort of
3 or something like that
4 and so on

e Add vague phrases to these sentences. (Sometimes there is more than one possible answer.)

1 This could be a reading corner with a bookshelf and a lamp.
2 We could use this shelf for herbs and spices and jars of jam.
3 There's a walk-in closet in the bedroom. We could use it for coats or shoes.
4 I could imagine a big plant over there by the window.

6 SPEAKING

a ≫ **Communication 7C** Student A go to p. 130. Student B go to p. 132.

b 💬 Show your room plans to the rest of the class. Who has designed the most interesting room?

☑ UNIT PROGRESS TEST

→ **CHECK YOUR PROGRESS**

You can now do the Unit Progress Test.

7D SKILLS FOR WRITING
There is a great deal of concern

1 SPEAKING AND LISTENING

a 💬 Discuss the questions.

1 What changes in urban development have you noticed in your local area? Think about things like new facilities (hospitals, schools), new roads, shopping malls, etc.

2 Do you think these examples of urban development are positive or negative? Why?

b ▶07.17 Listen to six people talking about a shopping mall planned for their local area. Is each person for (*F*) the plan, against (*A*) the plan, or do they have mixed views (*M*)?

1 Rene ☐   2 Susie ☐   3 Cecilia ☐

4 David ☐   5 Miles ☐   6 Marion ☐

c ▶07.17 Listen again. What reasons does each person give for his/her point of view? Take notes. Use the words/phrases in the box to help you.

| progress | living space | convenient |
| safe | the price you pay | part of a chain |

d 💬 How would you feel if a shopping mall was planned for your local area?

2 READING

a Read Rene's email to his friend Rosie about the planned shopping mall. What does he say in the email that he didn't mention in 1b?

Hi Rosie,

Thanks for your message. Great to hear from you. I'm glad your trip's going well.

The big news here is a shopping mall – would you believe it? Last Monday, the local government released their urban development plan, and it shows that a shopping mall's going to be built just across the road. My parents think it's a great idea, but I think it's going to be a disaster. It'll just mean a whole lot of the same horrible chain stores. And there'll be so much traffic!

But the thing that really makes me angry is that they aren't going to discuss this with people who live in the area. It looks like they're planning to just go ahead with building the mall. I'm sure they're not allowed to do that. Actually, I'm going to write an email to the local government and complain. I think a few people are planning to do that – maybe we can get them to change their minds.

I'd better get back to it. Hope you keep having fun!

Take care,
Rene

b Read Rene's email to the local government. What is the main reason for his complaint?

1 the problems the local community will have when the mall is built

2 the way the local government has communicated the plan for the mall

---

Subject: Planned Riverway Shopping Mall

To Whom It May Concern,

ᵃI am writing regarding the intention to build a shopping mall which was outlined in the urban development plan.

ᵇIn my neighborhood, there is a great deal of concern about the effect the mall will have on our local community. However, what worries us most of all is the fact that there has been no discussion with local residents. We understand that before a change of this nature can become part of a plan, a proposal needs to be sent out so residents can give feedback on it.

ᶜIn the past few days, I have tried to contact different local council members to find out how the plan was agreed to, but no one has returned my calls. I also visited your offices and asked to see the minutes of the meeting where the plan was discussed. I was told they were not available. The person I spoke to suggested that I should write this email.

ᵈI believe that what you are doing is against the law, and I would formally like to request that the local government withdraw the plan and put out a proposal that can be discussed with local residents.

ᵉIf I do not hear from you within two days, my next step will be to get in touch with the media. This will ensure there is a discussion of the plan in local media and also online.

I look forward to a prompt reply.

Best regards,
Rene Ferrer

---

c Read the email again. Answer the questions.

1 Who has Rene tried to speak to?

2 Who does he plan to contact next?

3 What does he want the local government to do? Why?

3 WRITING SKILLS Using formal language

a Match paragraphs a–e in Rene's email to the local government to the summaries below.

1 ☐ describes what action Rene has taken

2 ☐ explains his reason for writing

3 ☐ indicates why Rene is concerned

4 ☐ says what action he will take if there's no response

5 ☐ explains what action he wants the local government to take

b Compare Rene's informal email to Rosie with his formal email to the local government. What are the differences in … ?

- greeting
- sign-off
- punctuation
- contractions

c Find more forms of these expressions in the formal email.

1 I'm just getting in touch about …

2 Everyone's worried about what the mall will be like for us.

3 We think you should have sent out a proposal.

4 I think it's illegal and I want you to …

5 Get back to me in a couple of days or …

6 I want you to …

7 I can't wait to hear from you.

d Rewrite this informal email to make it more formal.

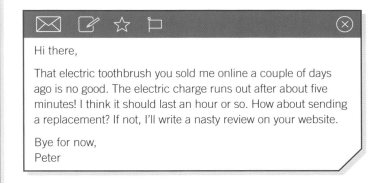

Hi there,

That electric toothbrush you sold me online a couple of days ago is no good. The electric charge runs out after about five minutes! I think it should last an hour or so. How about sending a replacement? If not, I'll write a nasty review on your website.

Bye for now,
Peter

e Compare with other students. Are your emails similar?

4 WRITING

a Work on your own. Choose a situation below to complain about or use your own idea.

- Your cell phone company has changed your contract without letting you know.
- Your electricity/gas/water company has charged you too much on your last bill.

b Take notes on:

- the background to the complaint
- what actions you have already taken
- your request for action
- what you will do next if no action is taken.

c 💬 Work in pairs. Tell each other about your situation. Help each other with ideas.

d Write your email of complaint. Use the structure and expressions from 3a–c.

e Work in new pairs. Read each other's emails. Did your partner include all the points in 4b? Do you think the person receiving the email will respond to the complaint?

UNIT 7
Review and extension

1 GRAMMAR

a Change the sentences to *had* or *got* + past participle.

Sara stayed at the Excelsior Hotel on a business trip. Her boss told her the company would pay the hotel bill.

1 She decided not to eat in the restaurant. *She asked them to bring all her meals to her room.*
   She had …
2 She called the laundry service. *They washed and ironed all her clothes.*
3 Then she went downstairs to the hairdresser. *They cut and dyed her hair.*
4 Then she went next door to the beauty salon. *They massaged her face and manicured her nails.*
5 The total cost was $3,500. *She asked them to add everything to her hotel bill.*

b What can you have (or get) done in these places?

1 a hairdresser's
2 a car mechanic's
3 a dental surgeon's
4 an optician's

c Andre is unhappy about his life. Add *too, too much, too many,* or *enough* to his sentences.

My faults …
1 I don't study.
2 I drink soda.
3 I don't go to bed early.
4 I'm not kind to my parents.
5 I don't get exercise.
6 I download movies.

d Connect these sentences using *so* or *such* and *that*. You may have to change some words.

1 It was a lovely day. We decided to go to the beach.
   It was such a lovely day that we decided to go to the beach.
2 There were a lot of people on the beach. We couldn't find a place to sit.
3 The water was cold. You couldn't go swimming.
4 We went to a café to eat but it was very expensive. We just ordered coffee.
5 It was very strong coffee. I couldn't drink it.

2 VOCABULARY

a Choose two words in the box for each sentence.

space   traffic   pollution   transportation
parking   air   congestion   public

1 Factories are a major cause of _____ _____.
2 I don't like driving into the city because I can never find a _____ _____.
3 We want to encourage people to leave their cars at home and use _____ _____.
4 The main problem in our city is _____ _____. It takes me two hours to drive to work in the morning.

3 WORDPOWER *down*

a Look at the pictures. What do you think is happening?

b Match the two halves of the sentences. Which sentences go with the pictures in 3a?

1 After he got married, he decided to stop traveling and
2 I've tried, but I can't find a job anywhere. It's starting to
3 Don't get so upset. Just have a drink of water and
4 They offered me a job in Quito, but I think I'll have to
5 I love all the birthday parties, but now I need to
6 My new boss thinks she's so important. She seems to

cut down on the cake.

calm down.

settle down.

look down on everyone.

turn it down.

get me down.

c Which multi-word verb means:

a stay in one place
b relax
c make (someone) feel depressed
d feel superior to
e refuse, say no
f decrease, lessen the amount.

d Complete the blanks with the correct forms of multi-word verbs in 3b.

1 She works 10 hours a day in a factory and earns almost nothing. Sometimes it really _____.
2 We've considered your offer, but we've decided to _____ as we've already made an agreement with another company.
3 OK, everybody, there's no danger, so please just _____ and don't panic.
4 I'm trying to _____ the amount of time I spend on social media.
5 Just because they're poor and they don't have a nice car like you, there's no reason to _____.
6 You've had too many part-time jobs! It's time to _____ and choose a career.

e 💬 Work in pairs. Choose a verb and talk about it. Can your partner guess the verb?

A I don't like our new neighbors. They always criticize people. They think they're better than everyone else …
B They *look down on* other people?

⟳ REVIEW YOUR PROGRESS

How well did you do in this unit? Write 3, 2, or 1 for each objective.
3 = very well   2 = well   1 = not so well

I CAN …	
discuss living in cities	☐
discuss changes to a home	☐
imagine how things could be	☐
write an email to complain.	☐

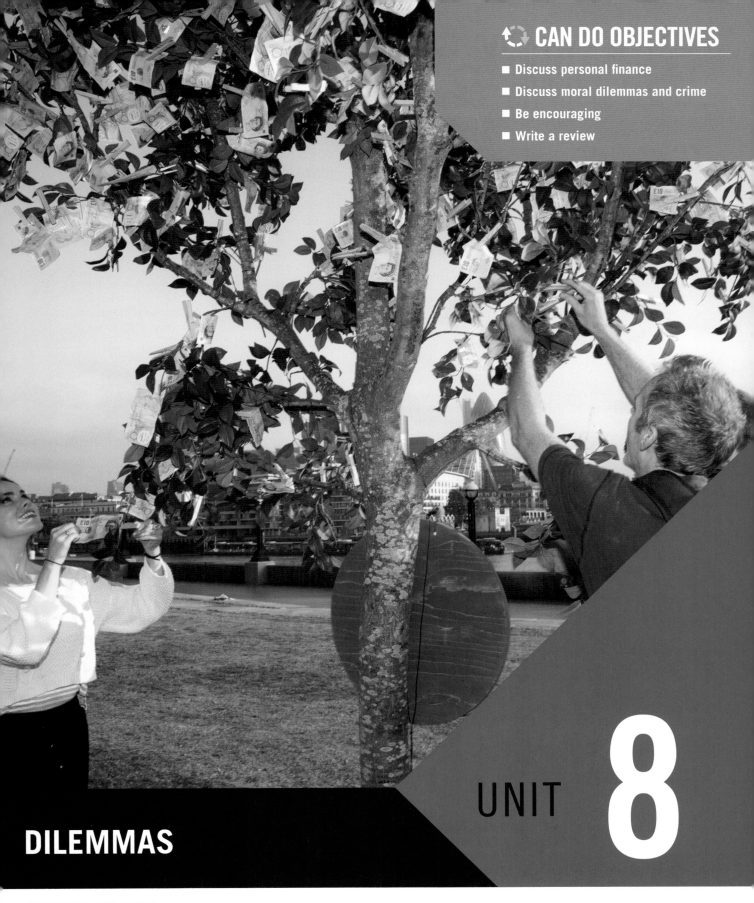

⟳ CAN DO OBJECTIVES

- Discuss personal finance
- Discuss moral dilemmas and crime
- Be encouraging
- Write a review

DILEMMAS

UNIT **8**

GETTING STARTED

a 💬🔊 Look at the picture and answer the questions.

1 What do you think is happening?
2 Do you think this is real money? Who put it there? Why?
3 If you had been there, would you have taken any money?

b 💬🔊 Discuss the questions.

1 There is a common expression in English, "Money doesn't grow on trees." What does this mean and when do people say it?
2 If money did grow on trees, do you think most people would be happier? Why / Why not?

8A | I'D LIKE TO START SAVING FOR A HOME

1 VOCABULARY Money and finance

a 💬🔊 Read the money facts below. Do any of them surprise you? Do you think these statistics are similar in your country? Why / Why not?

1 The U.S. population has a total credit card **debt** as high as $1 trillion.

2 50% of people don't know the **interest rates** on their credit cards.

3 57% of households in the U.S. don't have any kind of **budget**.

4 If you take a packed lunch to work every day, your **savings** can be about $1,500 a year.

5 3/4 of students will never fully **pay off** their student loans.

6 A survey in the U.S. showed that only 53% of people understand how to make an **investment**.

7 On average, people in the U.S. spend $1.33 for every $1.00 they make in **income**.

8 54% of people prefer to make **donations** to charity online rather than through mail or phone donations.

b Match the definitions with the words in **bold** in 1a.

1 a financial plan
2 to repay money you owe in full
3 money you give to help people or organizations
4 money that you owe
5 a fixed amount you have to pay when you borrow money
6 the amount of money you have saved
7 money that you earn or receive
8 money you put into a bank or business to make a profit

c Complete the sentences with the collocations in the box. Use the correct verb forms.

---
make / living   put aside / savings   award / grant
donate / charity   charge / account   finance / project
---

1 The university has decided to _____ the group a _____ of $10,000 for their research project.
2 Every month, the bank _____ my _____ about $15 in fees. It feels like robbery!
3 I don't know how he _____ a _____ from his café. He never has any customers.
4 Why don't you _____ the money to a _____ like Save the Children?
5 Local businesses agreed to _____ a _____ to increase the number of trees in the city's parks.
6 Since she started work, she hasn't _____ any _____. She spends all the money she earns.

d 💬🔊 Answer the questions and compare with other students.

- Do you or your family have a weekly or monthly budget?
- Do you or your family have a credit card? If so, do you know the interest rate?
- Do you ever donate money to charity? Do you pay in cash or online?
- Do you try to put aside savings? How often?
- Do students in your country have to pay off loans after they graduate?
- Have you ever made an investment in crowdfunding (supporting someone who is raising money for a unique goal)? Why / Why not?

2 LISTENING

a ▶ 08.01 Listen to a radio show about personal finance. Check (✓) the topics you hear.

1 ☐ saving for retirement   3 ☐ investment plans   5 ☐ student loans
2 ☐ credit card debt   4 ☐ paying off debt   6 ☐ personal spending

b ▶ 08.01 Listen again. Complete the chart.

	Jacob	Sophie
Caller's problem		
Mia's advice		

c Work in pairs. Do you agree with Mia's advice? Why / Why not?

3 GRAMMAR Future real and present / future unreal conditionals

a Match 1–3 with a–c to make sentences from the radio show.

1 ☐ If you transfer your card,
2 ☐ If I did that,
3 ☐ If I were you,

a I'd use the money to pay off your student loan.
b you'll probably pay as little as 3%.
c I wouldn't be able to afford things like new clothes and going out to dinner.

b Match the examples in 3a with these uses:

1 ☐ to give advice to someone
2 ☐ to talk about a situation we think is a real possibility
3 ☐ to talk about a situation that we think is imaginary or less likely to happen.

c Choose the correct explanation of the statements.

MIA If you transferred your card, you'd probably pay as little as 3%.
JACOB If I do that, I won't be able to afford things like new clothes and going out to dinner.

1 Jacob is talking about a different period of time.
2 Jacob thinks the situations are more or less likely.

d ≫ Now go to Grammar Focus 8A on p. 148.

e Are these situations real possibilities for you or not? Make future real conditional or present / future unreal conditional sentences for each one.

1 If I (get) a loan from the bank, I (be) able to buy a new car.
2 If I (put) aside $10 a week for a year, I (have) enough money to buy a new phone.
3 If I (want) to buy a new home, I (have to) borrow a lot of money from the bank.
4 If I (stop) buying my lunch for a week, I (donate) the money to charity.
5 If I (download) an app, I (have to) be careful not to make in-app purchases.

f 💬 Discuss your sentences. Did you use the same conditionals?

4 READING

a 💬🔊 Think of things you've bought in the past week. Tell each other what you bought and the different ways you paid.

b Read "Is it Time to Give Up on Cash?" What is the writer's aim?

1 to promote the benefits of a cashless society
2 to question some of the benefits of a cashless society
3 to give a balanced view of the benefits and drawbacks of a cashless society

c Read the article again. Match the headings with paragraphs 2–6.

A Sense of Reality	The Honesty of Cash
Were They So Wrong?	Better for Everybody
Almost Cashless Now	

d Read the article again. Answer the questions.

1 What's the evidence we're already in a cashless society?
2 What costs do businesses and consumers have when they use cash?
3 Why might you spend more when you use a credit card?
4 What does the psychological test tell us about the relationship between digital payments and honesty?
5 What does the writer suggest the overall effect is of a cashless society?

5 SPEAKING

a Work on your own. What's your opinion of these statements? Take notes.

1 The reason people get into financial trouble is that they're not taught how to manage personal finance. This needs to be introduced as a subject in school.

2 Financial experts tend to oversell the need to save money. They forget that people need to enjoy life and that often means spending money.

3 There are too many financial experts saying too much about personal finance. This doesn't help – it just creates confusion and people feel too much pressure.

4 A lot of people are so obsessed with their personal wealth that they forget about giving money to charities that can help people who are less fortunate.

b 💬🔊 Discuss the statements in 5a with other students. Explain your opinions. Do you all agree?

c Which advice do you think is the most relevant to you? Why?

IS IT TIME *TO GIVE UP ON CASH?*

¹If I asked you to put down this article and take out your wallet or purse, what would you find inside? There would probably be a few plastic cards there, but how many of you have any cash?

²For years now, economists have predicted a gradual move to what is called a "cashless society." Many payments are made using a card, and many more with phones or watches.

³So what's the attraction of a cashless world? Well, for one thing, cash is expensive. We often pay fees when we use cash machines – each person in the U.S. pays an average of $350 a year in cash-machine fees. Cash also spreads disease. Dr. Peter Ender, who carried out a study looking at the bacteria on one-dollar bills, claims that "paper money is usually full of bacteria and a dollar bill could, theoretically, be the magic carpet it rides on from one host to another." And of course, there's always a record of digital money, so it makes it harder for people to steal it. Businesses that handle large amounts of cash usually need to pay security companies to keep their cash safe, but you don't need a security guard to help you manage digital money.

⁴However, do we really save? Some psychologists question this. They argue that waving your debit card in front of a machine doesn't give us a real sense of spending money. Furthermore, when we make a quick payment online, it's easy to forget that the credit card bill will arrive at the end of the month. There's plenty of psychological research to show that when we pay using physical bills and coins, we spend more sensibly. Basically, with a credit card we don't feel the "pain of paying." In a cashless society, we tend to buy more than we need to because it's easier to spend and the consequences of our spending feel separate from us.

⁵And it's certainly still possible to cheat and steal in a cashless society. If you manage to cheat someone and you never have to look them in the eye, then it's easier to take the payment. In a psychological test, people were twice as likely to accept a dishonest digital payment as a dishonest cash payment. Once again, psychologists suggest that the sense of being separate from payment in a cashless scenario increased the likelihood of dishonesty.

⁶So, while we might laugh at the idea of our grandparents with money hidden under the mattress, maybe the joke is on us. In our bright, shiny, plastic, cashless society, maybe things are not as wonderful as we think they are. Perhaps it's a society that's not quite as honest as we'd like to believe. Without a doubt, it's a world where we feel removed from the consequences of the purchases we make. Reality arrives in the form of a large credit card bill at the end of the month. So perhaps we're more efficient in our cashless society, but are we any happier?

8B | I WOULD HAVE TOLD THE MANAGER

Learn to discuss moral dilemmas and crime

G Past unreal conditional; *should have* + past participle

V Crime

1 READING AND LISTENING

a 💬 Read about Alena and Roberto and discuss the questions.

1 Are their experiences typical or unusual? Why do you think so?
2 Have you (or someone you know) had an experience similar to Alena's or Roberto's? Tell other students about it.

ALENA I left my bag at the bus station. The next day, I received a call from the lost-and-found office. The bag had been turned in and everything was still there – wallet, cash, and cards.

ROBERTO I left my coat on a park bench with my wallet in it and when I went back, it was gone. A week later, the coat was turned in to the police. The wallet was still in it, but someone had taken all of my money and cards.

b Read the article "The Honesty Experiment." What did the researchers want to find out?

1 how honest hotel employees are
2 how honest people are worldwide
3 which cities have the highest rate of theft

c ▶08.03 Listen to three people saying what they would have done. Which person would have … ?

1 thought about keeping the money in the wallet
2 let their manager deal with the problem
3 refused to take the wallet

d ▶08.03 Listen again. What is the main point that each speaker makes? Choose a or b.

Speaker 1
a You shouldn't take money that isn't yours.
b The person who lost the money was careless.

Speaker 2
a You can't expect people in low-paid jobs to be honest.
b If you return a wallet to someone, it's OK to keep some of the money for yourself.

Speaker 3
a It could be risky to accept a wallet from a stranger.
b The police should take responsibility for stolen money.

e ⫸ **Communication 8B** Go to p. 131 and find out what researchers discovered. Then answer the questions.

1 What do the results seem to show about people's honesty?
2 Why do you think people don't want to "see themselves as a thief?"
3 Do you think this was a reliable test of honesty? Why / Why not?

The Honesty Experiment

Imagine you're a receptionist at a hotel. A tourist walks in and tells you they found a lost wallet outside the hotel but they're in a hurry, and they ask you take care of it. What do you do? Do you try to return the wallet to the owner and does it make a difference if the wallet has money in it?

A team of researchers recently decided to conduct an "honesty experiment" involving more than 170,000 "lost" wallets in 335 cities in 40 different countries. The researchers handed the wallets to employees at banks, post offices, hotels, and movie theaters and said they had been found on the street outside. Each wallet contained a grocery list and business cards with an email address. Some of them had no money, some had about $10 in cash, and others had around $90.

So how would people react? Would they return the wallet with the money to the owner, would they keep it all, or would they take some of the money?

2 GRAMMAR
Past unreal conditional; *should have* + past participle

a Look at these examples and answer the questions.

If I'd been an employee at the hotel, I would have told the manager.
I certainly wouldn't have taken the money.

1 Are the speakers … ?
  a talking about something that really happened
  b just imagining a situation

2 Are they talking about … ?
  a the present   b the future   c the past

3 Complete the rules for the past unreal conditional:

With *if* clause:
_____ + _____
With main clause:
would + _____ + _____
  a *have* + past participle   b *if* + past perfect

b Look at these examples and choose the correct answers.

Obviously, the person **should have been** more careful.
He **shouldn't have dropped** the wallet.

1 The **bold** expressions are used:
  a to say something was possible
  b to criticize someone.

2 The form of the **bold** expressions is:
  a *should(n't)* + present perfect
  b *should(n't)* + *have* + past participle.

c ▶ 08.04 **Pronunciation** Listen to these sentences. The stressed words are in **bold**.

He **shouldn't** have **dropped** the **wallet**.
You **should** have **told** me.

What do you notice about the pronunciation of the unstressed words?
Are they … ?
1 the same length as the stressed sounds
2 shorter and said more quickly

Practice saying the sentences.

d ⫸ Now go to Grammar Focus 8B on p. 148.

e What would you have done if someone had given you the wallet? Would you have … ?
- checked the contents and then contacted the owner
- given it to your manager or boss without opening it
- kept the money and thrown the wallet away
- refused to take the wallet

3 SPEAKING

a Work in two pairs. You are going to read about two "moral dilemmas." Pair A: Read "The Bribe" and answer the questions. Pair B: Go to p. 130.

1 Read the story and answer the questions.
  a Why was George stopped?
  b Why did they want him to sit in the police car?
  c Why did he pay them?
2 What do you think George should have done? Why?
3 What would you have done?

George Manley, his wife and two children were driving home late at night from a winter vacation. They were in a hurry to get home because their four-year-old son had a high fever, so George was driving over the speed limit. Suddenly, he saw the flashing blue and red lights of a police car behind him. The police car stopped them, and because it was a cold night, the officers asked him to bring his ID and proof of insurance and come and sit in the police car. Then, to his surprise, they told him he would need to go to the police station to pay the fine and this would take several hours because the police station was about 50 km away. Instead, they said that George could simply pay them in cash and he could drive on with no delay; they would fill in the forms at the police station the next day. He knew he was being asked to pay a bribe, but he was worried about his son, feeling sick and increasingly desperate to get home to bed. He paid the money and told his wife what happened as he drove home. She agreed that he did the right thing in order to get their son home as quickly as possible.

b 💬 Work with a student who read about the other dilemma. Take turns talking about your stories. Do you agree with each other's ideas?

4 VOCABULARY Crime

a Which of the words in the box could you use to discuss ... ?

1 the test described in "The Honesty Experiment"
2 the two dilemmas in 3a

burglary theft lying robbery cheating bribery murder

b Answer the questions about the words in 4a.

1 Which words describe ... ?
- crime
- dishonest behavior which is not illegal

2 Three of the words mean "stealing money or valuable things." Which means ... ?
a stealing in general
b stealing from a home or a building
c stealing with violence (e.g., with a knife or a gun)

c Complete the chart with the correct words in the box.

cheat kidnapping thief burglary shoplift
bribe liar rob murder kidnapper robbery
shoplifter murderer

Person	Behavior/Crime	Verb
a burglar	_____	burglarize
a _____	theft	steal
a robber	_____	_____
a cheater	cheating	_____
a _____	lying	lie
	bribery	_____
a _____	murder	_____
a _____	_____	kidnap
a _____	shoplifting	_____

d Read the news headlines and choose the correct word.

Bank *burglars* / *robbers* escape with $500,000 after police are forced to give up search

Car *kidnapping* / *theft* is increasing, say police

Detectives solve *murder* / *lying* mystery after years of investigating

10% of college students *cheat* / *burglarize* on tests, report claims

Two teenagers sent to prison for *shoplifting* / *cheating*

Burglars / *Kidnappers* stole items worth more than $50,000 in three months

e ⟫ Now go to Vocabulary Focus 8B on p. 161.

5 SPEAKING

a 💬 Read the situations. What would you have done?

- "I saw my friend stealing something in the grocery store. Of course I didn't tell anyone – she's my friend."
- "A colleague in my office lied about the company accounts. I was the only one who knew he was lying. I sent my manager an anonymous note."
- "During my final exam in college, I saw a student look at answers on a small piece of paper. I didn't say anything. It didn't have anything to do with me."

b Which of these situations do you think is the most serious? Why?

c Do you think it's always important to be honest?

8C EVERYDAY ENGLISH
You'll find something

Learn how to be encouraging
Ⓢ Showing you have things in common
Ⓟ Word groups

1 LISTENING

a 💬🔊 Discuss the situations below.

1 If a friend or family member has a bad day, how do you try to cheer that person up?
2 When was the last time you tried to cheer someone up?
  a What was the situation?
  b How did they react?

b Look at the photo of Serena and Natasha. What do you think Natasha is doing at her computer?

c ▶08.10 ▶08.11 Listen to Parts 1 and 2. What is going on with Natasha and Serena?

1 Natasha just heard that she ... .
  a lost her job
  b didn't get a new job
2 Serena's about to ... .
  a give a presentation
  b start a new job

d ▶08.10 ▶08.11 Listen to Parts 1 and 2 again. Are the sentences true or false?

Part 1
1 Craig told Natasha she didn't get the job.
2 Natasha didn't prepare for the interview.
3 Natasha is going to send out more résumés.

Part 2
4 Serena is job hunting.
5 Serena is dressed up for an interview.
6 Serena wants to impress someone.

2 USEFUL LANGUAGE
Being encouraging

a Look at these two excerpts from Part 2. Underline the expressions where Natasha or Serena are being encouraging.

1 **NATASHA** Oh, job hunting, you know …
  SERENA Yeah, it's never easy. Don't give up hope – you'll find something.
2 **SERENA** I hope so!
  NATASHA I'm sure you will. Good luck.

b Look at these expressions for being encouraging for 30 seconds.

1 It might work out fine.   3 I'm sure it'll be fine.
2 Never give up hope.   4 You never know.

Now cover the expressions and complete the conversations below.

A I have my performance review with my boss tomorrow.
B You've had a good year. I'm _____ it'll _____ fine.
A I'd like a pay raise, but I don't think I'll get it.
B Well, you _____ know.

C It's our final game of the season tomorrow and two members of our team can't play. We're bound to lose.
D It _____ work _____ _____.
C But they're our two best players.
D Never _____ up _____.

c ▶08.12 Listen and check.

d 💬🔊 Work in pairs. Take turns having short conversations like in 2b. Use expressions to be encouraging.

Student A: Tell your partner about a grammar test you have tomorrow. You're worried that you haven't studied enough.
Student B: Tell your partner about a speaking test you have next week. You don't think your pronunciation is good enough.

3 LISTENING

a ▶08.13 Listen to Part 3. Natasha and Craig talk about Natasha's news. How have their experiences been similar?

b ▶08.13 Listen again and answer the questions.

1 What job did Natasha get?
2 When does Natasha start?
3 Why does Craig have to end the conversation?

4 CONVERSATION SKILLS
Showing you have things in common

a ▶ 08.13 In Part 3, Natasha and Craig share experiences they have in common. For example, Natasha says:

The same thing happened to me!

Listen again and find two more expressions that show they have things in common.

b Look at the expressions below. Do we use them before or after someone mentions their experience?

1 The same thing happened to me.
2 I've just had a similar experience.
3 I know the feeling.
4 It was just like that when …
5 It was the same with me.
6 That's just like when …

c Cover 4b and correct the mistakes.

1 It was same with me.
2 I've had the similar experience.
3 I know a feeling.
4 It was just so when …

d 💬 Tell each other about your experiences learning English. Say when you have something in common.

5 LISTENING

a ▶ 08.14 When Natasha checks her phone, she finds a voicemail message. Listen to Part 4 and answer the questions.

1 Who's the message from?
2 What's it about?
3 What's the telephone number?

6 PRONUNCIATION Word groups

a ▶ 08.15 Listen again to the message. Add // where the speaker pauses.

Hello, Natasha. It's Jessica here from Media Makers. Thanks for coming in to interview earlier. A new position has just come up and we think you might be right for it. Can you call me back at 555-249-4566?

b Why does the speaker use pauses? Choose the correct description.

1 She needs to stop and think about what she's going to say next.
2 She wants to make sure the information in her message is clear.

c Work alone. Think of a message you can leave for your partner. Decide where you need to pause to make the message clear.

d 💬 Work in pairs.

Student A: Give a message to Student B.
Student B: Listen and write Student A's message. Switch roles.

7 SPEAKING

a Think of a hope you have but are unsure about. For example, it could be:

- a vacation
- a job
- a study goal
- a place to live.

b 💬 Take turns talking about your hopes. Encourage your partner and show that you have something in common if they talk about similar experiences.

I don't know if I can afford to travel this summer.

Yeah, it's never easy. But you can stay in a hostel.

I've heard the job interviewing process is pretty hard.

Yes, I know the feeling. But you're good at interviews …

✓ UNIT PROGRESS TEST

➡ CHECK YOUR PROGRESS

You can now do the Unit Progress Test.

1 SPEAKING AND LISTENING

a 💬 What TV shows do you enjoy watching? What do you like about them? What don't you like?

b 💬 The credit card statement below was the focus of a crime that was featured on a reality TV crime show. What do you think could have happened?

CREDIT CARD STATEMENT

ACCOUNT NUMBER	DUE DATE
256-6658-1153	07/01

TRANSACTION DATE	DESCRIPTION	AMOUNT
06/02	Senior bus pass	36.00
06/03	Groceries	69.00
06/04	Dentist	25.00
06/05	Jewelry	150.00
06/05	Purse	120.00
06/05	Women's clothing	300.00
06/05	Women's shoes	220.00
06/06	Women's clothing	130.00
06/07	Women's clothing	280.00
	TOTAL:	1,330.00

c ▶ 08.16 Listen to Paul and Zadie talk about the TV show. Were any of your ideas in 1b correct?

d ▶ 08.16 Listen again. Are the sentences true or false?

1 Paul thinks the show teaches people how to commit crimes.
2 The man's niece went looking for the credit card statement.
3 Zadie isn't sure the niece did the right thing.
4 The man talked about how frightened he was by the theft.
5 Paul didn't like the attitude of the host.
6 Zadie thinks the show could be seen as useful advice.
7 Paul thinks the host had an original point of view.

e 💬 Discuss the questions.

- Do you know of any crimes similar to this? Or any famous crimes? What happened?
- Do you think these TV shows teach people how to commit crimes? Why / Why not?

Crime with a Smile

2 READING

a Read the book review "Crime with a Smile." Is the series fact or fiction?

b Read the review again and complete the chart.

author	
characters	
setting	
kind of story	
reason for liking	
why it's recommended	

Janet Evanovich

¹I like a good crime story, but sometimes they are too serious. They often take you into the mind of the criminal and can be too intense. So, I was delighted to find a crime novelist who makes me laugh. Janet Evanovich is a best-selling author whose Stephanie Plum series is hilarious. If you enjoy classic crime stories that are also humorous, you must read this series.

²Stephanie Plum is a bounty hunter who hunts down criminals and then gets a reward for finding them. Sometimes, she gets asked to do very unusual jobs. I just finished reading book 25 in the series, *Look Alive Twenty-Five*, and it's my new favorite. Stephanie and her business partner, Lula, take over running a delicatessen. Why? The last three managers vanished, leaving behind only one shoe each. Stephanie has to figure out what happened while making sure she doesn't disappear, too. Lula is on hand to help and so is Stephanie's on-again, off-again boyfriend, cop Joe Morelli.

³One of the things I really like about *Look Alive Twenty-Five*, and the whole series, is the way the story revolves around great characters. There is the key group – Stephanie, Lula, Joe, Vinnie, Stephanie's boss who's always in a bad mood, as well as her live-in grandmother, Grandma Mazur, who refuses to grow old. They're all funny and lovable. Each book introduces more characters who are equally entertaining. The other thing I like about the series is that the crime doesn't always involve a murder. People don't need to die to create a sense of mystery and excitement. Evanovich is great at building the action, so you are pulled into the story and you can't put the book down.

⁴So if you're looking for a break from the typical crime story and you want to read crime-with-a-smile, I highly recommend *Look Alive Twenty-Five*.

3 WRITING SKILLS
Organizing a review

a Read the book review again. Choose the correct endings for the descriptions of paragraphs 1–4.

1 ☐ This introduces the book and gives …
2 ☐ This outlines the plot and introduces …
3 ☐ This outlines the key strengths of the book and the reviewer's …
4 ☐ This is a summary of the review and a final …

a positive recommendation.
b personal opinion.
c information about it.
d the main characters.

b Underline phrases in the review in 2a that show the writer's positive opinion of the book.

c Notice how the words and phrases in the box are alternatives to the language used in the review. Complete the sentences with the words and phrases in the box. Sometimes more than one answer is possible.

love	should	enjoy
really	number one	

1 … you _____ read this series.
2 This is my new _____.
3 One of the things I really _____ about *Look Alive Twenty-Five* is the great characters.
4 The other thing I _____ about the series is that crime doesn't always involve a murder.
5 I _____ recommend it.

4 WRITING

a Think of a book, movie, or TV show that you like and would recommend. Take notes using the chart in 2b.

b Work on your own. Write your review. Organize the review clearly, using the advice in 3a. Include your positive opinions, using language in 3b and 3c.

c Work in pairs. Read each other's reviews and check that each paragraph has a clear purpose and the paragraphs are in the right order. Check the correct use of positive expressions.

d Switch your review with other students. Would you like to read the book or watch the movie or TV show you read about?

1 GRAMMAR

a Complete the sentences with your own ideas.

1 If I go out tonight …
2 If I went to a very expensive restaurant …
3 If I buy some new clothes this weekend …
4 If I bought a new IT device …
5 If I download some new music …

b 💬 Discuss your sentences.

c Read about Sam's disastrous night out.

As he went out, he forgot to lock the front door and some burglars stole all of his electronic equipment. He didn't put any gas in his car, so he ran out and had to pay for a taxi home. He didn't check the name of the club he was going to, so he couldn't meet his friends. He put his phone in his back pocket and it was stolen.

Imagine a different night out for Sam with sentences beginning with *if*. For example:

If he'd remembered to lock his front door, he wouldn't have been burglarized.

d Make sentences criticizing Sam. Begin each sentence with *He should/shouldn't have* …

2 VOCABULARY

a Put the letters of the <u>underlined</u> words in the correct order.

1 Every month I work out the <u>dteugb</u> for household expenses.
2 My weekly <u>ceinmo</u> is just over $500, and I don't think it's nearly enough.
3 They borrowed money from the bank and have a <u>bdte</u> of $8,000.
4 I have a new credit card that has a very low <u>eernitts</u> <u>eatr</u> on payments.
5 Last year, I made a total of 12 <u>oonndasti</u> to different charities.
6 We've just <u>daip fof</u> a loan from my parents so we can start saving for a home.

b Write the correct noun form of the verbs in parentheses in the blanks.

1 There have been a lot of _____ (burglarize) in our neighborhood lately.
2 Police charged the man with _____ (steal) and sent him to jail to wait for a trial.
3 She's a _____ (cheat) and is always copying my ideas and work.
4 There was a real problem with _____ (bribe) and corruption in the local government.

3 WORDPOWER *take*

a Connect a sentence from 1–6 to another from a–f.

1 ☐ There seems to be no one who's responsible for the project.
2 ☐ You may not believe what the advertisements say, but this chocolate tastes great.
3 ☐ My friends tell me not to worry about the test.
4 ☐ I love the food she makes because she's such an enthusiastic chef.
5 ☐ It's done nothing but rain since we arrived. It's making me feel so depressed.
6 ☐ I didn't read the conditions on the ticket carefully.

a You can tell she takes pleasure in what she makes.
b I took it for granted that we could get a refund easily.
c But I take all assessments seriously and make sure I study hard.
d Take my word for it.
e I can't take it for much longer.
f I'm more than happy to take charge.

b Answer the questions about the *take* expressions.

1 Which word can be replaced with the word *control*?
2 What preposition follows these expressions: *take interest, take pride, take pleasure*?
3 What's the problem with this example? *We take seriously all security matters.*
4 What's the problem with this example? *Please believe me – take the word for it.*
5 Which expression is followed by *that* + clause?

c Add a *take* expression where you see ^. Think about the verb form and word order.

I always ^ that my friends ^ in the hiking trips I used to organize. I was happy to ^ of all the preparation. However, one of my friends, Julia, admitted that no one was really that interested in going hiking except me. Julia was very diplomatic when she said that it was important to ^ people's different interests. However, another friend, Shelley, was far more direct. She said, "I'm sorry, but I ^ it any longer – I've had enough of hiking!" Well, we won't be going hiking ever again – ^ !

d 💬 Discuss your answers to the questions.

1 What do you take pleasure in?
2 Are you someone who likes to take charge? Why / Why not?
3 What's something you take seriously?

↻ REVIEW YOUR PROGRESS

How well did you do in this unit? Write 3, 2, or 1 for each objective.

3 = very well   2 = well   1 = not so well

I CAN …	
discuss personal finance	☐
discuss moral dilemmas and crime	☐
be encouraging	☐
write a review.	☐

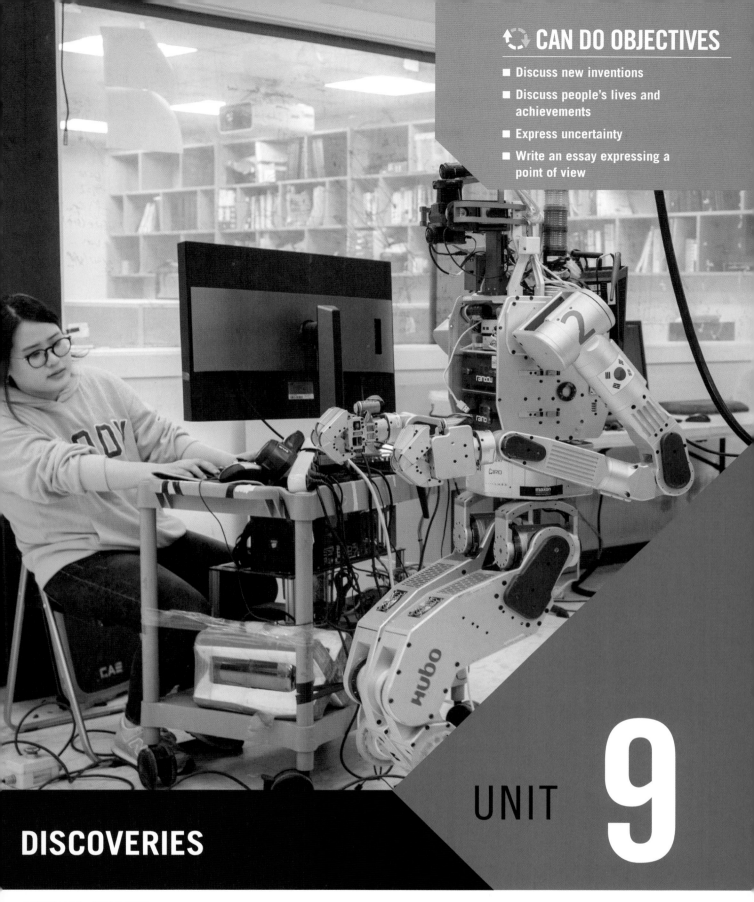

⟳ CAN DO OBJECTIVES

- Discuss new inventions
- Discuss people's lives and achievements
- Express uncertainty
- Write an essay expressing a point of view

UNIT 9

DISCOVERIES

GETTING STARTED

a 💬🗩 Look at the picture and answer the questions.

1 What is the person at the computer doing?
2 What do you think this robot is capable of?

b 💬🗩 Discuss the questions.

1 Imagine you could have a robot built for you. What would you want it to do? Why?
2 Do you think new inventions and discoveries always lead to an improved quality of life? Why / Why not?
3 Do you think there are things people will always want to do themselves (instead of machines)? Which ones? Why?

1 READING

a Read "Medical Science or Science Fiction." Do you think the inventions are fact or fiction?

b Read the article "Too Good to Be True?" Which of the inventions in 1a are real?

Too Good to Be True?

We're always hoping for the next medical miracle – like a simple pill that can cure cancer. Often we hear of breakthroughs in medical science that sound almost too good to be true. However, sometimes they really are as good as they say they are. Here are five inventions from the world of medical science. If they sound like science fiction, that just means that the future is here – now.

1 Black and White

Wouldn't it be great if people who had lost their sight could see again? This is already happening for some blind people. A small device is put in the back of a blind person's eye. They then wear special sunglasses with a camera, which transmits images to the device. It isn't a perfect system, but it's enough for them to be able to walk down the street or to know the difference between black and white socks.

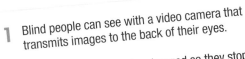

MEDICAL SCIENCE OR SCIENCE FICTION?

80%

1 Blind people can see with a video camera that transmits images to the back of their eyes.

2 A person's genes can be changed so they stop eating food that makes them overweight.

3 Hospital patients can wear electronic skin to send radio waves from their body to machines.

4 During an operation, it's likely that a computer tablet will take care of you.

5 Medical scientists are close to finding a vaccine against the common cold.

6 It'll soon be possible to prevent people from suffering from food allergies.

7 Electronic devices placed in the chests of asthma sufferers can permanently cure the illness.

8 A small electronic device put in the brain of an epilepsy sufferer can stop them from having seizures.

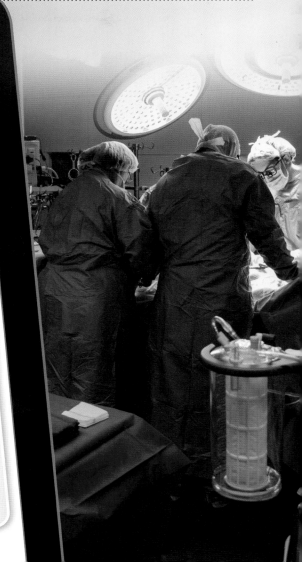

c Read the article again. Are the sentences true or false?

1 Anyone who's blind is able to get sight back with the new glasses and see perfectly.
2 Electronic skin can be used to monitor patients and speed up the healing process.
3 The tablet now means that the anesthetist can leave the patient once the operation begins.
4 Scientists hope that it will be possible to turn off other allergies in the future.
5 The epilepsy device has two functions: prediction and prevention.

d 💬 Discuss the questions.

1 Which of the inventions do you think is the biggest breakthrough in medical science? Why?
2 Imagine a medical invention you would like to exist. What would it do? Why would you like it to be real?

2 VOCABULARY Health

a Underline the medical verb in each example. Then match the verbs with definitions 1–3.

… simple pill that can cure cancer.
It can also be used to help heal wounds …
… a computer tablet will take care of you.

1 treat a disease and make healthy again
2 provide treatment
3 treat an injury and make healthy again

b Complete the sentences with the correct form of the verbs in the box.

get   develop   strain   come   treat

1 I feel terrible. I've _____ down with the flu.
2 His doctor _____ his throat infection with antibiotics and that helped.
3 I can't stand up for very long because I've _____ my back.
4 I don't want to go out yet. I'm still _____ over a major cold.
5 People who eat too much fatty food are likely to _____ heart disease.

2 It's All About Comfort

In hospitals, patients often complain about all the uncomfortable cables and wires that connect them to monitors. It's now possible to get rid of all this wiring simply by putting on electronic skin. This piece of "skin" is very small and very thin. It's about the size of a postage stamp and as thick as a piece of human hair. It's made of silicon and is attached using water in the same way that a fake tattoo is. Despite being extremely small and thin, the skin contains electronic circuits that can receive and send radio waves to and from monitors. It can also be used to help heal wounds by sending out heat that speeds up the repair process.

3 Under the Care of Three

During an operation, there's always a surgeon in the operating room and an anesthetist, whose job is to check the patient constantly. In the past, the anesthetist had to watch the patient carefully, but these days they are also likely to use a touchscreen computer like a tablet. This tablet monitors key functions like breathing and heart rate, but more importantly, it can send the anesthetist warnings and suggest how medication should be altered during the operation. It also keeps a record of everything the surgeon does. So these days, when you have an operation, you're under the care of three "professionals:" the surgeon, the anesthetist, and the tablet.

4 Sometimes a Matter of Life and Death

It's surprising how many people are allergic to different kinds of food. Sometimes this can be life-threatening, for example, for people who are allergic to peanuts. Scientists at Northwestern University in Chicago have found a way to turn off an allergy to peanuts. They attached some peanut protein to blood cells and reintroduced them into the body of someone suffering from the allergy. This makes the body think that peanuts are no longer a threat and there's no allergic response. Scientists think this approach could be used with a wide range of food allergies.

5 Warning Signs

People who suffer from epilepsy never know when they are going to have an attack. This lack of certainty can be very stressful. Researchers have now created a device that makes an epileptic seizure predictable. These very small devices are planted in the brain. They're able to tell if an attack is about to happen, and they can then send out electrical signals to other parts of the brain that can stop the seizure.

c Match verbs 1–5 with the pictures. Two verbs describe one picture.

1	cough	2	faint	3	sneeze
4	pass out	5	shiver			

d 💬 Discuss the questions.
- When did you last come down with the flu?
- What do you think is the best way to treat a sore throat?
- Have you ever fainted? What happened?
- Have you ever strained a muscle? Which muscle? How did it happen?
- What serious disease or illness are people in your country most likely to develop?

e ⋙ Now go to Vocabulary Focus 9A on p. 162.

3 LISTENING

a ▶09.03 Listen to Teo and Rosie talk about inventions. Which medical invention and which food invention do they talk about?

b ▶09.03 Listen again and answer the questions.
1 What did the scientist do with the meat?
2 Why's this meat better for the environment?
3 What does Rosie suggest that Teo do to reduce crop production?
4 What does Rosie say about the taste of the meat?
5 Why does Rosie think it's strange that Teo's worried about global warming?

c Whose point of view do you agree with more, Teo's or Rosie's?

4 GRAMMAR Relative clauses

a Underline the relative clause in each sentence. Decide if it adds information about a thing (T), a person (P), or a place (PL).
1 Yeah, there's this laboratory where they're growing meat. PL
2 There was that scientist who made his own hamburger and ate it online.
3 But all these tiny pieces of meat that they have to push together just to make one burger.
4 And the end result is something that costs $250,000.
5 There's no fat or blood in it, which means no flavor.
6 I mean, these scientists, who are like Dr. Frankenstein, how can they justify that?

b Answer the questions about the clauses you underlined in 4a. Which clauses … ?
1 add extra information that is not necessary to the overall meaning of the sentence
2 are necessary for the sentence to make sense

c ⋙ Now go to Grammar Focus 9A on p. 150.

d 💬 Discuss what you think about the following inventions. Do you think they have been useful for people in general? When do you use them? Could people manage without them now?
- cameras
- plastic
- antibiotics

5 SPEAKING

a ⋙ **Communication 9A** Student A: Go to p. 132. Student B: Go to p. 131.

b 💬 Put the inventions in order of usefulness from 1–4 (1 = very useful, 4 = completely useless). Discuss your ideas with the class.

9B THEY HAD NO IDEA IT WAS A FRAUD

1 READING

a 💬 Look at the reports and discuss the questions.

> The airport was closed after a bomb scare, but it turned out to be a **hoax**.
> They thought it was painted by Monet, but it was a **fake**.
> The manager of the company was arrested for **fraud**.
> If you receive an email asking you to check your bank account, it's almost certainly a **scam**.

1 What do all the remarks have in common?
2 What do the words in **bold** mean?
3 How common do you think fraud is in your country? What forms does it take?

b Read the article "The Rise and Fall of Barry Minkow" and answer the questions.

1 What was Barry Minkow's job?
2 How did Minkow "rise"?
3 How did Minkow "fall"?

c Read the article again and take brief notes on the following.

- how Barry Minkow made money at the beginning
- the second company Minkow set up
- the people and organizations that Minkow made money from

Compare your notes with another student. Did you write the same things?

d Read the sentences about what happened to Barry Minkow later. Three of the sentences are true. Which do you think they are? Give reasons for your choice.

1 He stayed in prison less than 10 years.
2 He completely changed his character.
3 He became a pastor in a church.
4 He was sent to prison again.

e ≫ **Communication 9B** Now go to p. 132. Did you guess correctly?

The Rise and Fall of Barry Minkow

At the age of 16, Californian Barry Minkow launched his own carpet cleaning company from his parents' garage. He was so successful that, only four years later, the company was listed on the American stock market with a value of $280 million, making Barry Minkow a multi-millionaire and also the youngest CEO of a public company in American history. But a few years later, he resigned from the company and was sentenced to 25 years in prison. So what went wrong and how did his phenomenal success turn to disaster?

The answer is that although Barry Minkow seemed like a successful entrepreneur, he wasn't able to run a profitable business. Instead he focused on getting money for his company in any way he could.

When he started his carpet-cleaning business, called *ZZZZ-Best*, he raised money by engaging in credit card fraud, stealing his grandmother's jewelry and even arranging fake "robberies" at his office to get insurance money.

Later he set up a second company, which specialized in restoring buildings damaged by flooding or fire, with the work paid for by insurance companies. In fact the company was a fake: the buildings didn't exist and the documents and contracts were forged. However, he convinced the banks that he was running a successful business and got them to lend him more money, which enabled him to expand *ZZZZ-Best* and turn it into a public company. But Barry Minkow's past was finally catching up with him.

An article in the *Los Angeles Times* claimed that Minkow had been involved in false credit card charges and that only those who had noticed the false charges had got their money back. Shortly after that, investigators reported that his second company was a fake and that its "restoration" jobs didn't actually exist. After Minkow suddenly resigned "for health reasons", the new directors discovered that he had stolen $230 million from the company before he left.

A year later he was charged with fraud and sentenced to 25 years in prison.

2 GRAMMAR Reported speech; reporting verbs

a Look at these examples of things people said.

> Minkow **was** involved in false credit card charges.

> Only those who **noticed** the false charges **got** their money back.

> His second company **is** a fake.

> Its "restoration" jobs **don't** actually **exist**.

These statements are reported in the sentences below using reporting verbs. Complete the sentences with the correct form of the verbs in parentheses. Then check your answers in the text.

1 An article in the *Los Angeles Times* <u>claimed</u> that Minkow_____ (be) involved in false credit card charges.
2 The article also <u>claimed</u> that only those who _____ (notice) the false charges _____ (get) their money back.
3 Shortly after that, investigators <u>reported</u> that his second company _____ (be) a fake.
4 They also <u>said</u> that its "restoration" jobs _____ (not/ actually/exist).

b Complete the rule with the correct answers.

> Because the reporting verbs (*said, claimed, reported*) are in the *present / past*, what the people said moves "one tense back" into the *present / past*.

c Look at these examples of questions people asked or thought.

> Is he really the reformed character that he claims to be?

> What's going on?

> Where is our money really going?

Complete the reported questions with the correct form of the verbs in parentheses. Check your answers in the text.

1 Very few people questioned whether he _____ (be) really the reformed character that he claimed to be.
2 Some people began to wonder what _____ (be) going on and where their money _____ (really/go).

> Choose the correct word to complete the rule:
> In reported questions, *use / don't use* question word order.

d ≫ Now go to Grammar Focus 9B on p. 150.

e Correct the mistakes in these sentences.

1 Investigators weren't sure whether Barry Minkow is telling the truth.
2 They asked him if he can show them the company accounts.
3 People at the church didn't understand why did he steal money from them.
4 Customers were asking will they ever get their money back.

3 LISTENING

a Imagine you receive the email subject below.

From: health@importantinfo.gov
Subject: WARNING! Dangerous bananas

How would you react? Would you think ... ?
1 That sounds serious and I eat bananas. I'd better see what it says.
2 It sounds like a hoax, but it could be serious.
3 It's probably a scam. I'll delete it without opening it.

What do you imagine the email might say?

b ▶09.07 Listen to two people talking about the email. Check (✓) the topics that they mention.

☐ poison   ☐ bacteria   ☐ Central America
☐ restaurants   ☐ monkeys   ☐ grocery stores
☐ talk shows

How are the topics you chose connected?

c ▶09.07 Listen again and answer the questions.

1 Is the Centers for Disease Control and Prevention a real place?
2 In what sense were the bananas supposed to be "man-eating"?
3 Why did the news about the bananas spread so quickly?
4 What effect did this have?
5 How common is necrotizing fasciitis?
6 How was the story in Africa different from the one in the U.S.?

4 VOCABULARY
Verbs describing thought and knowledge

a Look at the sentences from the discussion. Which verbs in the box can you use instead of *thought* or *knew* to make the meaning more precise? Put them into the correct form.

assume come to the conclusion
have no idea realize suspect

1 Maybe they *thought* it was a hoax but they weren't sure. (= think or believe something is true but be uncertain about it)
2 People *didn't know* what "necrotizing fasciitis" was. (= not know at all)
3 They started discussing it on TV talk shows, and eventually people *thought* it was just a hoax. (= decide after thinking about it)
4 It sounded like a reasonable story, so I guess people just *thought* it was true. (= believe something is true without questioning it)
5 So everyone stopped eating bananas from South Africa for a while, until they *knew* it was all a hoax. (= suddenly understand)

b ▶09.08 Listen and check your answers.

c Write possible continuations to these sentences. Think carefully about the correct verb form to use.

1 After getting to know her better, I came to the conclusion …
2 It was already 5:30. He realized …
3 After working for the company for six months, I started to suspect …
4 Our next-door neighbor seemed very ordinary. We had no idea …
5 You didn't answer when I called, so I assumed …

5 SPEAKING

a Think of an example of a hoax, scam, or case of fraud that you know about. It could be:
- a hoax designed just for fun
- an email or Internet scam
- a case of fraud that happened in your country or in another country.

b 💬 Work with a partner. Think about how you will describe what happened and take brief notes. Try to include reported speech and verbs from 4a.

c 💬 Tell other students about your topic.

Learn how to express uncertainty

P Linking and intrusion

S Clarifying a misunderstanding

Megan

Pam

1 LISTENING

a 💬🔊 Discuss the questions.

1 When was the last time you had a surprise?
2 Was it a good or bad surprise? What happened?
3 Do you usually like surprises?

b Look at photo a and answer the questions about Pam and Megan.

1 Does Megan look excited about where Pam is taking her?
2 Does it look like Megan knows where they are?

c ▶09.09 Listen to Part 1. Check your ideas in 1b.

d 💬🔊 What do you think the surprise is? Discuss your ideas.

2 USEFUL LANGUAGE
Expressing uncertainty

a ▶09.10 Read the conversation below. Is it what Megan and Pam said? Listen and check.

MEGAN I don't know where we are.
PAM Just wait and see.
MEGAN Where are we going?
PAM Wait and see.

b In which version does Megan express herself more strongly? Why does she do this?

c Megan talks about a place: "I have no idea where we are."

Look at these expressions for talking about a thing.

1 I (really) have no idea what that is.
2 I don't have a clue what that is.
3 What in the world is that?

Change expressions 1–3 to talk about a person.

d ≫ **Communication 9C** Student A: Go to p. 133.
Student B: Go to p. 131.

3 LISTENING

a 💬🔊 Look at photo b and answer the questions.

1 Where do you think Pam and Megan are going?
2 Do you think Megan will like the surprise?

b ▶09.11 Listen to Part 2 and check your ideas in 3a.

c ▶09.11 Listen again. Answer the questions.

1 Did Pam buy tickets?
2 What doesn't Megan like?
3 Did Megan like Pam's surprise? Why / Why not?
4 What did Pam misunderstand?
5 What do Pam and Megan decide to do?

4 PRONUNCIATION Linking and intrusion

a ▶09.12 Listen to an excerpt from the conversation. Pay attention to the underlined phrases. Do they sound like separate words or one word?

MEGAN You're <u>not annoyed</u>?
PAM No, <u>not at all</u>.
MEGAN Maybe we can <u>grab a bite</u> instead.
PAM <u>Good idea</u>!

b Why are the sounds connected? Choose the correct description.

1 All the vowel sounds in these words are short sounds.
2 Final consonant sounds are followed by vowel sounds.
3 There is no stress in any of these phrases.

c ▶09.13 Listen to the excerpt. Notice the phrases with ⌢. Where are the sounds in the box added?

/j/ /r/ /w/

MEGAN I have no ⌢ idea where we ⌢ are. I've never seen this street before.
PAM Just wait and see.
MEGAN Where ⌢ in the world are we going?
PAM Wait and see.

d Why do we add the sounds in 4c? Choose the correct explanation.

1 The main stress is on the word that comes after each added sound.
2 The consonants in the two words are voiced.
3 The last sound in the first word and the first sound in the following word are both vowels.

e ▶09.14 Using the rules from 4b and d, predict where the speaker is going to use linking and intrusion. Then listen and check.

Here at work, I just received a gift from my aunt. I have no idea what it is. I'm going to open it when I go home tonight.

5 CONVERSATION SKILLS
Clarifying a misunderstanding

a ▶09.15 Listen to part of Megan and Pam's conversation. Which two expressions does Pam use to clarify a misunderstanding? (Both expressions begin with *but*.)

b Look at the conversations. Which are social situations? Which are work situations? <u>Underline</u> the expressions in B's replies used to clarify misunderstandings.

1 **A** I'm off to the movies now.
  B I thought that you were going to a soccer game.
2 **A** Our next meeting's in two weeks.
  B I understood that we were going to meet once a week.
3 **A** Here's your ticket. It's $50.
  B Did I get this wrong? I thought it was free.
4 **A** By the end of this month, you'll be able to take a week's vacation.
  B Did I misunderstand something? I thought I could take two weeks of vacation.
5 **A** How about if I make the appetizer and you make the dessert?
  B Didn't we say that I'd make the appetizer?

c What could you say in the situations below? Write your ideas and compare with your partner.

1 You're in a restaurant. Your friend told you he/she wasn't hungry but has ordered an appetizer, a main course, and a dessert.
2 You stay in a hotel. When you pay the bill, you're surprised to find breakfast is extra.
3 A friend offers you a ride to the station. When you get in, he/she starts driving in the opposite direction.

6 SPEAKING

a ≫ **Communication 9C** Student A: Go to p. 130. Student B: Go to p. 131.

✅ UNIT PROGRESS TEST

➡ CHECK YOUR PROGRESS

You can now do the Unit Progress Test.

1 SPEAKING AND LISTENING

a 💬🔊 Discuss the questions.

1 Do you think alternative treatments really work or do you think people just imagine that they work?
2 What kinds of alternative medicine are common in your country?
3 If you were ill, would you try alternative medicine? Why / Why not?

> **Alternative medicine** Kinds of medical treatment that use different methods from standard Western medicine (also called *conventional medicine*). Examples of alternative medicine are homeopathy, herbal medicine, and acupuncture.

b ▶️ 09.16 Listen to people talking about four alternative treatments. What treatment does each person talk about? Match them with photos a–d.

c ▶️ 09.16 Listen again and answer the questions for all the speakers.

1 Why did the person try this treatment?
2 What did the doctor/therapist do?
3 Does the speaker feel positive or negative about it?
4 Do we know if the treatment worked?

2 READING

a Read Alicia's essay "The Value of Alternative Medicine." Which sentence best summarizes her argument?

1 Conventional medicine is more effective, but alternative medicine may be useful sometimes.
2 Alternative medicine is often more effective than conventional medicine, so it should be used more widely.
3 Conventional and alternative medicine work in different ways and both of them are important.

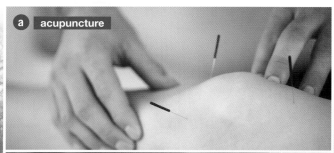
a acupuncture

b homeopathy

c herbal medicine

d hypnosis

The Value of *Alternative Medicine*

People often have extreme points of view about alternative medicine. People who believe in conventional medicine often argue that alternative medicine is of no use at all, and supporters of alternative medicine sometimes claim that it can replace conventional medicine completely.

b Look at the points that Alicia makes in her essay. Which are about conventional medicine and which are about alternative medicine? Write *C* or *A*.

1 ☐ It has been used for a very long time and in many different countries.
2 ☐ It is often cheaper.
3 ☐ It may have harmful side effects.
4 ☐ We can't show scientifically that it works.
5 ☐ People who use it often say it works.

3 WRITING SKILLS
Presenting a series of arguments

a Alicia's essay in 2a has five paragraphs. What is the purpose of each one? Complete the sentences.

1 In the first paragraph, she outlines …
2 In the next three paragraphs, she presents …
3 In the final paragraph, she summarizes …

b Find six expressions in Alicia's essay which introduce arguments and points of view.

People often argue that …

c Alicia uses linking words and phrases to show how her ideas are connected. Find words and phrases that mean:

1 also (x2)   2 but   3 so   4 although
5 finally

d Choose one of the topics below and think about your point of view. Write three sentences about the topic, using expressions from 3b and 3c.

- Are zoos cruel to animals?
- Does dieting make people fat?
- Do video games cause bad behavior in young people?
- Is love a good basis for marriage?
- Should smoking be made illegal?

4 WRITING

a Think again about the topic you chose in 3d. Plan an essay using the structure in 3a. Think about:

- how you will introduce the topic
- what arguments you will present and what examples you will give to support them
- what conclusion you will give.

b Write the essay in around 200 words.

c Switch essays with your partner. Read the essay. Does it … ?

- have a clear introduction and conclusion
- present the arguments clearly, with a separate paragraph for each main idea
- include examples to support the arguments
- use appropriate expressions to introduce the arguments

d 💬 Work in new pairs. Read another student's essay. Then say if you agree with his/her point of view and why.

There are several good reasons for taking alternative medicine seriously. First, many forms of alternative medicine, such as acupuncture and herbal medicine, have a very long tradition and are widely used in many parts of the world. It's important not to ignore traditional knowledge that has been used and developed for centuries.

One argument against alternative medicine is that there is very little scientific evidence to prove that it is effective. Yet, in spite of the lack of scientific evidence, people who use alternative therapies generally say that they work. This suggests that alternative therapies may perhaps work in ways that we do not yet fully understand. Furthermore, people are often willing to spend a lot of money on alternative treatment, despite the fact that it is often not covered by insurance, so it can be more expensive than conventional medicine.

In addition, unlike the drugs and antibiotics used in conventional medicine that can be harmful to the human body, most alternative therapies are completely harmless. Homeopathic treatments, for example, have few or no side effects, and consequently the worst that can happen is that they have no effect at all.

In conclusion, I believe that conventional medicine and alternative therapies should exist side by side. They work in completely different ways and are often effective for different kinds of illnesses, so they should both be seen as a useful way to keep us healthy.

Review and extension

1 GRAMMAR

a Connect the sentences using a relative clause. Use a relative pronoun if it's necessary. Cut any unnecessary words.

1 The bandage is like a piece of skin. The bandage is very small and thin.
2 The skin contains electronic circuits. The circuits can communicate with monitors.
3 An operating room is a sophisticated environment. Patients require extra care in an operating room.
4 People with severe peanut allergies have to check the ingredients for everything they eat. Some people are severely allergic to peanuts.

b Tell the story, changing the parts in *italics* into indirect speech, using reporting verbs.

I was on a business trip, and I had a terrible time getting back home. My flight was at 12:30. But when I arrived at the airport, they announced:
[1]"*There has been a delay to the incoming flight, so the flight will be delayed by about an hour.*" After an hour, we still hadn't heard anything and I started to wonder, [2]"*What's happening?*" I asked one of the flight attendants, [3]"*Do you know when the flight will leave?*" She told me, [4]"*I haven't heard anything.*" I waited for two more hours. At about 5:00, they told us, [5]"*The flight has been canceled.*" I realized, [6]"*I'll have to spend the night in an airport hotel, and I probably won't be home for another 18 hours.*"

2 VOCABULARY

a Choose the best word in these sentences.

1 Some scientists *estimate / realize* that there are 100 billion stars just in our galaxy.
2 I'm sorry I didn't say anything. I didn't *assume / realize* it was your birthday.
3 I followed you because I *doubted / assumed* that you knew the way.
4 I *wonder / come to the conclusion* how much she earns in a month. It must be at least $10,000.
5 As I left the apartment, I *doubted / was aware* that someone was following me, and I was fairly sure I knew who it was.

b Add words from the box to the blanks.

| patients strained feel back lost dizzy |
| scar care consciousness heals |

1 I _____ _____. I think I'm going to faint.
2 It hurts when I try to stand up. I think I've _____ my _____.
3 She's a student nurse. She takes _____ of _____ in the hospital, and she also has to study for exams.
4 They hit me on the head and I _____ _____.
5 When the wound _____, it will probably leave a _____.

3 WORDPOWER *come*

a Match the sentence beginnings and endings.

1 Her dream was to see the ocean, and last month her dream **came**
2 I think we should go to the movies, unless you can **come**
3 Look, there's a photo of you in the paper. I **came**
4 The restaurant was pretty expensive – the check **came**
5 I thought about buying the car for a long time, but I **came**
6 We were talking about who to ask, and your name **came**

a **across** it this morni
b **true**.
c **to** more than $250
d **up** as a possible person.
e **to the conclusion** t I couldn't afford it.
f **up with** a better ide

b Match the expressions in 3a with the definitions.

a see something by chance
b think of
c be mentioned
d add up to
e reach a decision
f really happen

c Choose the correct words or phrases.

1 "OK – two coffees – that comes *to / up* $9.50."
2 At the meeting, we came up *to / with* lots of new ideas.
3 Nuclear power is a topic that often comes *true / up* in students' essays.
4 We thought about going to Paris, but we came *to / across* the conclusion that Rome would be nicer.
5 I came *across / to* a fascinating article in this magazine. It might interest you.
6 I always wanted to own a BMW, and now my dream has finally come *true / across*.

d Complete each question with one word.

1 Do you know anyone whose dream came _____?
2 Have you ever been given a check that came _____ more than you could afford?
3 Have you ever come to the _____ that something you bought was a waste of money?
4 How do you feel if someone says, "Your name came _____ in our conversation?"
5 Many people come _____ with new ideas when they're falling asleep or going for a walk. Is that true of you?
6 Have you ever come _____ a bargain in a store or a market that you couldn't resist?

e 💬 Ask and answer the questions in 3d.

⟳ REVIEW YOUR PROGRESS

How well did you do in this unit? Write 3, 2, or 1 for each objective.
3 = very well   2 = well   1 = not so well

I CAN ...	
discuss new inventions	☐
discuss people's lives and achievements	☐
express uncertainty	☐
write an essay expressing a point of view.	☐

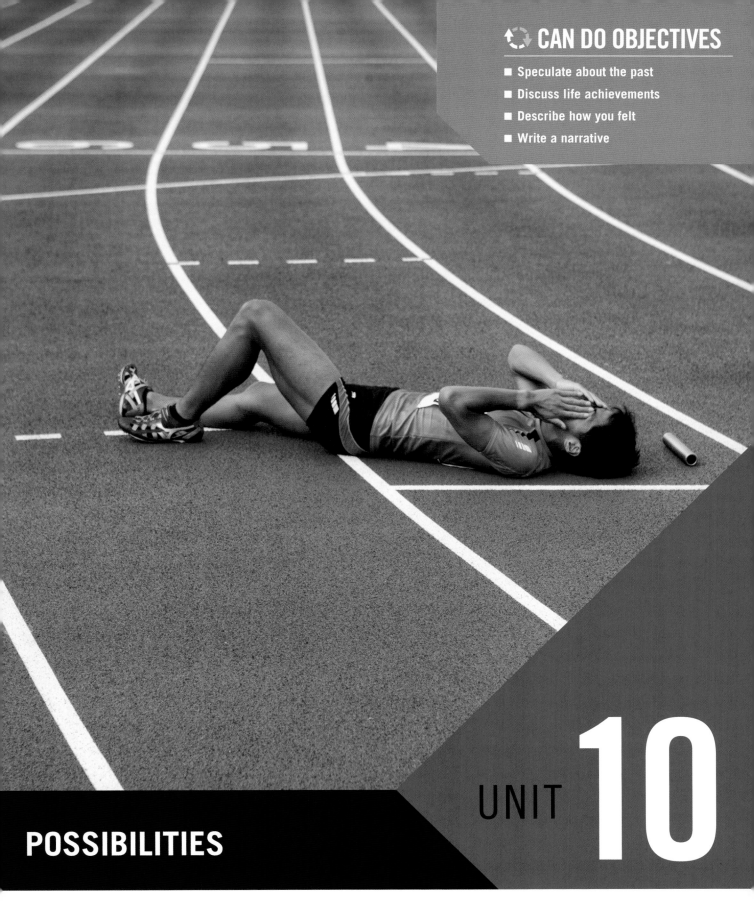

↻ **CAN DO OBJECTIVES**

- Speculate about the past
- Discuss life achievements
- Describe how you felt
- Write a narrative

UNIT 10

POSSIBILITIES

GETTING STARTED

a 💬🎤 Look at the picture and answer the questions.

1   What has just happened to this man?
2   What is he thinking? What is he feeling?

b 💬🎤 Discuss the questions.

1   When people have high ambitions, what kinds of expectations do they have of themselves?
2   Do you think people are sometimes unrealistic in setting goals for themselves? Why?
3   What are the positive and negative consequences of having high expectations of yourself?

10A | IT MIGHT NOT HAVE BEEN HIS REAL NAME

1 READING

a You are going to read a story about Dan Cooper, who mysteriously disappeared in 1971. Look at the pictures of people and events in the story. Can you guess what happened?

b Read "The Man Who Disappeared" quickly. How similar is it to your ideas?

c Find sentences in the story that show:

1 the flight from Portland to Seattle was a short one
2 we're not sure if Dan Cooper was the man's real name
3 the passengers didn't know about the note or the bomb
4 Cooper told the pilots to fly toward Mexico as slowly and as low as possible
5 the pilots didn't want to leave the rear door open
6 the pilots knew when the rear door was opened.

d 💬 Discuss the questions.

- What questions would you like answered that are not explained in the text?
- Do you think Cooper survived? What would you prefer to believe, that he survived or that he didn't survive? Why?

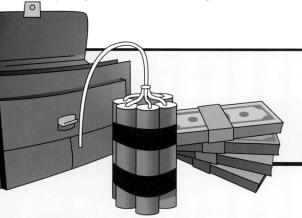

The Man Who DISAPPEARED

Flight attendant Florence Schaffner was sitting in her seat during takeoff. A man in a seat near her passed her a note. It read, "I have a bomb in my briefcase. I will use it if necessary. Sit next to me."

It was 2:50 p.m. on November 24, 1971, on Flight 305, a 30-minute flight from Portland to Seattle in the northwest U.S. And it was the beginning of one of the strangest stories in the history of plane travel – a mystery that remains unsolved to this day. The man's name – or at least, the name he gave when he bought his plane ticket – was Dan Cooper. Of course, this might not have been his real name; no one really knows for sure.

Schaffner quietly got up and sat next to the man. He opened his briefcase slightly, and she glimpsed eight red sticks inside before he closed it again. Then Cooper made his demands: $200,000 (a huge amount of money in 1971), four parachutes, and a fuel truck ready at Seattle Airport to refuel the plane. The attendant told the pilot, who passed the demands on to the airline company, and they agreed to them. The other passengers were told there was a "technical difficulty" and the plane circled for almost two hours over the ocean to give the airline time to get the money and parachutes ready.

Cooper was told that his demands had been met, and the plane landed at Seattle-Tacoma airport at 5:45 p.m. The money (in $20 bills) and the parachutes were delivered, and the passengers and Schaffner left the plane. Cooper talked to the pilots and ordered them to fly toward Mexico at minimum speed and altitude, with a refueling stop in Reno. The plane, a Boeing 727, had a door at the back that opened downward –

Cooper ordered the pilots to leave it open all the time. They objected, so Cooper said that he would open it himself when they were in the air.

After refueling, the plane took off at approximately 7:40, with Cooper and four crew members on board. After take-off, Cooper told the lone flight attendant to go to the cockpit. As she went, she saw him tie something around his waist, which may have been the bags of money. At eight o'clock, a warning light went on in the cockpit, so they knew that he must have opened the rear door. The plane landed in Reno at 10:15, with the rear door still open. Police searched the plane immediately, but they quickly confirmed that Cooper was gone.

Cooper was never seen again, dead or alive. No one has even found out if he really was Dan Cooper. And many people say that he couldn't have survived the jump (if indeed he jumped – he could have hidden on the plane and then escaped later) but no body, or parachute, was ever found. A bag with almost $6,000 of the money was found in a river, but the rest never showed up. The money might have belonged to Cooper, but even that wasn't certain.

Fifty years later, the crime remains unsolved – and it will probably remain that way forever.

DAN COOPER

2 GRAMMAR Past modals of deduction

a Match sentences 1–5 with meanings a–d.

1 ☐ He tied something around his waist, which **may have been** the bags of money.
2 ☐ Many people say that he **couldn't have survived** the jump.
3 ☐ It **might not have been** his real name.
4 ☐ He **could have hidden** on the plane.
5 ☐ A warning light went on in the cockpit, so they knew that he **must have opened** the door.

a It seems certain that this was the case.
b It seems certain that this was not the case.
c It's possible that this was the case. (x2)
d It's possible that this was not the case.

b Look at the examples in 2a again.

1 Complete the rule with the modal verbs in the box.

| must   may   might   couldn't   could |

To speculate about things in the past:
- we use _____ or _____ + *have* + past participle to talk about things we think are certain.
- we use _____, _____, or _____ + *have* + past participle to talk about things we think are possible.

2 Choose the correct answer, a or b.
- *Must* and *couldn't* mean a) the same b) the opposite
- *May*, *might*, and *could* mean a) the same b) the opposite

3 In the examples, *have* is:
a part of the present perfect tense
b an infinitive form which always stays the same.

c ▶10.01 **Pronunciation** Listen to the sentences. <u>Underline</u> the stressed syllables in each sentence.

1 He couldn't have survived the jump.
2 It might not have been his real name.
3 He must have opened the door.

Practice saying the sentences.

d ≫ Now go to Grammar Focus 10A on p. 152.

e Read these situations. What do you think happened? Use past modals of deduction to discuss each one.

1 Renato Nicolai was in his garden in the south of France when he heard a whistling sound and saw what he thought was an experimental aircraft. He watched as it dropped out of the sky, hovered about two meters off the ground, then rose into the sky and disappeared. When experts studied the place where it had come down, they found a "black material" on the ground that was not oil.

2 A ship called *The Joyita* disappeared in the Pacific without sending a call for help. It was found a month later floating in the ocean with no one on board. The lifeboats and the food were missing. There was a hole in the side, but it wasn't serious and the engines weren't damaged. The crew was never found.

3 LISTENING

a ▶10.03 Listen to an interview about Dan Cooper's disappearance. Number the topics in the order you hear them. There is one extra topic that you do not need.

the river ___
Dan Cooper's "wife" ___
airport security ___
the pilot of the Boeing 727 ___
the parachute ___
the money ___

b ▶10.03 What evidence is there for the opinions below? Listen again and check.

1 Dan Cooper wasn't his real name.
2 He worked in the aircraft industry.
3 He survived the jump.
4 He didn't survive the jump.
5 Someone helped him.

c What do you think might have happened?

4 READING

a What famous event is shown here? What's happening in the picture?

b Read the blog "Ten Amazing Coincidences" and answer the questions.

1 Which came first, the *Titanic* disaster or the book *The Wreck of the Titan*?
2 What is unusual about the book?

c Read the blog again. Which of these features of the book were similar to the *Titanic* disaster? Write *Yes*, *No*, or *Don't know*.

1 the name of the ship ___
2 the type of ship ___
3 the number of passengers ___
4 the description of the ship ___
5 where and when it sank ___
6 the reason it sank ___
7 how many people were rescued ___

d Discuss these three opinions about the blog. Which do you agree with the most? Why?

> It's amazing. Morgan Robertson must have been able to see into the future in some way.

> It might have been just a coincidence, but it's very difficult to explain it.

> It's not so extraordinary. Morgan Robertson must have known that large ships were being built and that icebergs were a danger.

5 VOCABULARY
Adjectives with prefixes

a Find adjectives in the blog in 4b which mean:

1 you can't believe it (x2)
2 it's not likely
3 it's not possible
4 it didn't sell many copies
5 it's not part of the main point.

What do all these adjectives have in common?

b ≫ Now go to Vocabulary Focus 10A on p. 163.

6 SPEAKING

a ≫ **Communication 10A** You are going to read two more stories from the series "Ten Amazing Coincidences." Student A: Go to p. 130. Student B: Go to p. 133.

BLOG | REVIEWS | GIVEAWAYS | ABOUT

Ten Amazing Coincidences
The Wreck of the Titan
by Morgan Robertson

Morgan Robertson Writes About the *Titanic* ... 14 Years Early!

A hundred years before James Cameron made the movie *Titanic*, American author Morgan Robertson wrote an unsuccessful book called *The Wreck of the Titan* about the sinking of an ocean liner. It's a story that's been told many times, and 13 movies have been made about it.

The Incredible Thing Is ...
Robertson's *The Wreck of the Titan* was published in 1898; that's 14 years before the *Titanic* was even built.

The similarities between Robertson's work and the *Titanic* disaster are really improbable. The *Titan*, like the *Titanic*, was described as "the largest craft afloat," "like a first class hotel," and "unsinkable." Both ships were British-owned steel vessels, they were both around 800 feet long, and they both sank after hitting an iceberg in the North Atlantic, in April, "around midnight."

What's Even More Unbelievable
In the novel, the *Titan* crashed into an iceberg 400 miles from the coast of Canada at 25 knots. The real-life *Titanic* crashed into an iceberg 400 miles from the coast of Canada at 22.5 knots. If you think of the size of the Atlantic, about 40 million square miles, that's such a close guess it seems impossible that Robertson didn't know in advance what was going to happen.

The Weirdest Thing of All
But maybe the weirdest thing about the *Titan* were details that were irrelevant to the story, but match what happened to the *Titanic*. For example, both the *Titan* and the *Titanic* had too few lifeboats to take every passenger on board. But it's an odd point to mention in the book when you consider that lifeboats had nothing to do with the story. In the book, when the *Titan* hit the iceberg, the ship sank immediately – so why did Robertson mention the lifeboats? Was it just coincidence, or did he somehow know what was going to happen?

b Tell each other your story. Do you think the events are coincidences, or is there some other explanation for what happened? Do you know any other stories like these?

10B | I'VE MANAGED TO MAKE A DREAM COME TRUE

Learn to discuss life achievements

G Wishes and regrets
V Verbs of effort

1 LISTENING

a Read quotes a–c about believing in your dreams. Which one do you like the most? Why?

> **a** "Work hard and dream the biggest dream you can – you'll see amazing things happen!"

> **b** "Dreams are all about what's going to happen tomorrow. Don't let your dreams get in the way of being the best person you can be – right here, right now."

> **c** "You need dreams when life gets boring or difficult – they're what get you out of bed in the morning and keep a smile on your face."

b 💬 What do you think is the most important ingredient in realizing your dreams? Why?

believing in yourself   hard work   knowing the right people   luck   money

c ▶ 10.05 Listen to Louise and Terry. They both decided to pursue their dreams. Match the speakers with the photos. They both made one change that was the same. What was it?

d ▶ 10.05 Listen again. What reasons do Louise and Terry give for making their change?

e 💬 What do you think happened next to Louise and Terry?

f ▶ 10.06 Listen to the second part of their stories. Were your predictions correct?

g ▶ 10.06 Listen again. Complete the chart.

	What problems did he/she experience?	What regrets does he/she have?
Louise		
Terry		

h 💬 Would you do what Louise and Terry did? Why / Why not?

119

2 GRAMMAR
Wishes and regrets

a Look at these examples from Louise and Terry's conversation. Who says each one?

1 If only I'd applied for his job when it became available.
2 I found it too crowded. I wish I'd checked this before leaving.
3 I should have checked out other companies.

b What are the speakers doing in the examples in 2a? Are they … ?

1 wishing for a change in their life
2 expressing regrets for things they have done
3 expressing regrets for things they didn't do

c Complete the rule.

To express regret about the past, we use:
1 *I wish* or *if only* + *I* + ___
2 *I should have* + ___

d ▶ 10.07 **Pronunciation** Listen to the examples in 2a. Notice the linking sounds. Which two words in each example are stressed?

1 If‿only I'd applied for his job
2 I wish‿I'd checked this
3 I should‿have checked out other companies

e ▶ Now go to Grammar Focus 10B on p. 152.

f Think of something you did in the past with mixed results (some parts were good, but others weren't). What would you do differently now? Take notes.

g 💬🎙 Tell each other about your past experiences and regrets.

3 READING

a Do you agree with the statement below? Why / Why not?

If you want a personal dream to come true, you need to focus on yourself and not think about other people. You will only be successful if you are determined in this way.

DREAM TO HELP

Many people have a dream or a goal in life. It's often something very personal that people want to achieve for themselves. However, some dreams include the idea of helping other people. Meet two people who have done just that.

Brandon Stanton

What Was His Dream?
Brandon wanted to be a professional photographer who could get his photographs published and maybe even have a best-selling photography book. He also wanted to stop being too concerned with money and focus more on helping people.

How Did His Dream Come About?
In 2010, Brandon Stanton was living in Chicago and working as a bond trader. He lost his job when his company went bankrupt. He decided to give up his career in the world of finance and came up with the idea of traveling around the United States to follow his real passion: photography.

Before losing his job, Brandon had been taking photos of downtown Chicago. He knew these photos weren't wonderful, but he felt he had potential as a photographer. Some would say it wasn't a smart move – risking your livelihood on your hobby. But Brandon thought, "If I don't do this now, I never will," and he decided to pursue his dream.

How Did He Achieve His Dream?
After traveling to different cities in the U.S., Brandon had the crazy idea of photographing 10,000 people in New York. Initially, he'd photographed streets and buildings, but when he started taking photos of people, he realized the portraits were getting more likes on Facebook. He had to overcome his fear of approaching strangers to ask if he could take their photos. He made himself do it and just kept on taking more and more portraits.

Eventually, he moved his portrait shots to his own website, which he called *Humans of New York*. He also started talking more to the people he was taking photos of and adding captions to the photos that explained something about the person's life. He realized these captions were as important as the photos themselves. Every day he worked on building his website, and after just a few months, his project took off and he had a million fans and a deal to publish a book. In 2013, *Humans of New York* came out and became an instant bestseller. But Brandon was determined not to use his fame just for himself.

He has used his website to help numerous charities. For example, in 2016, after photographing and sharing the stories of children at the Memorial Sloan Kettering Cancer Center in New York, he organized a campaign that raised over $3.8 million. He has also continued to do charity work and raise money for disadvantaged people in many of the countries that he has visited.

Brandon never forgot his early days in New York when he felt incredibly lonely and wondered if he would ever achieve his dream. But he stuck with it and made his dream a reality.

b 💬 Work in two groups and read the introduction. Group A reads about Brandon Stanton and group B reads about Michelle Javian. Decide with your group if you think Brandon or Michelle would agree with the statement in 3a.

c Read the text again and take notes about your person.

d 💬 Work with a student from the other group. Tell each other about your person. Decide which person you admire the most. Give a reason.

e Both individuals in the article made a dramatic change to follow their passion. How important do you think it is to do that? What type of person does it take?

Michelle Javian

What Was Her Dream?

Michelle wanted to set up and run a nonprofit organization that helps heart patients and their families. She wanted to be able to offer these people practical help during critical times in their illness.

How Did Her Dream Come About?

In 2008, Michelle's father had a heart transplant. She spent hours beside his bed in the hospital. During this time, she began to realize how difficult life is for families who have someone in cardiac care, particularly if they have to travel from out of town.

Sadly, Michelle's father passed away. She felt that the best way to honor his memory and cope with her sadness was to set up a nonprofit organization that gives practical support to families of people who are unwell because of heart disease.

How Did She Achieve Her Dream?

While looking after her father in the hospital, Michelle made friends with Yuki Kotani, whose father was also having a heart transplant. They talked to doctors and social workers and got a lot of ideas for the best way they could help people in similar situations. The health professionals suggested that providing affordable housing for the families of heart patients was the most effective way of reducing the stress of patients and their families. This led to Michelle and Yuki setting up a charity called Harboring Hearts.

Michelle had given up her job in the corporate world to jump into non-profit work. She didn't have previous experience in that area, so it was a huge challenge for Michelle to tackle. She quickly realized that the best way to raise money was by talking to people and telling her story. Donations began to come in, and before long she was able to help a family with four-year-old twin boys who both needed heart transplants.

In the beginning, it was extremely hard for Michelle because she hadn't gotten over her father's death. She felt as if she was just managing to put one foot in front of the other. However, thinking about her father also gave her the energy to not give up.

Harboring Hearts now works with a range of partner hospitals in New York, and they help up to 140 families a year. They have also begun organizing community events where heart patients can connect with and get support from people in the community who have been through a similar experience.

Michelle is very proud of what she has achieved – founding a charity organization that has such a positive impact on heart patients and their families. It's a real safety net for families who need it.

4 VOCABULARY Verbs of effort

a Notice the **bold** verbs in these examples from "Dream to Help." They are connected with the idea of making an effort to do something. Match the verbs with their meanings.

1 ☐ "If I don't do this now, I never will," and he decided to **pursue** his dream.
2 ☐ He had to **overcome** his fear of approaching strangers to ask if he could take their photo.
3 ☐ Every day he **worked on** building his website, and after just a few months, his project took off.
4 ☐ But he **stuck with** it and made his dream a reality.
5 ☐ She felt that the best way to honor his memory and **cope** with her sadness was to set up a nonprofit organization.
6 ☐ She didn't have previous experience in that area, so it was a huge challenge for Michelle to **tackle**.
7 ☐ However, thinking about her father also gave her the energy to not **give up**.

a to succeed in controlling difficult circumstances
b continue trying hard to do something difficult
c try to achieve something, usually over a longer period of time
d spend time doing something to improve it
e try to do a difficult task
f stop doing something
g manage to live with something even though it's difficult

b Replace the verbs/phrases in *italics* with the correct form of the **bold** verbs/phrases in 4a.

1 When was the last time you had to *succeed in controlling* a difficult work or study problem?
2 What's something that you do regularly and wouldn't want to *stop doing*?
3 In your free time, is there something you're *spending time to improve*?
4 What's a personal goal in your life that you are *trying to achieve over time*?
5 How well do you *manage* in emergency situations?
6 What's a work or study problem you *tried hard to solve*?
7 Do you have a difficult task you're *trying to do* at the moment?

c 💬 Ask and answer the questions in 4b.

5 SPEAKING

a Think of someone you know who has done something you think is brave or amazing.

He/She could be:
- a relative
- a family friend
- a colleague
- someone well known in your country.

Take notes on this person's background and his/her achievement.

b Tell each other about the people you chose. What similarities are there between them?

10C EVERYDAY ENGLISH
Two things to celebrate today

1 LISTENING

a 💬🗣 Discuss the questions.

1 When was the last time you celebrated something?
2 Was the celebration for yourself or for someone else?
3 How did you celebrate?

b Look at the photo. What do you think the professor and student are talking about?

c ▶10.10 Listen to Part 1. Check your ideas.

d Answer the questions with the adjectives in the box.

upset   pleased   surprised   worried

1 How does Maya feel at first?
2 How does she feel after she hears the news?
3 How does the professor feel? Why?

e ▶10.11 Listen to Part 2. Which of these things are they celebrating?

1 It's Hector's birthday.
2 Ruby is moving to Spain.
3 Ruby got her dream job.
4 Hector got into law school.
5 Hector got a new job.

f ▶10.11 💬🗣 Answer these questions. Listen again if necessary.

1 How did Maya feel about Ruby's news?
2 Why does Hector thank Ruby and Maya?

2 PRONUNCIATION
Consonant groups

a ▶10.12 Look at the words below. The underlined consonant sounds are pronounced together. We call these "consonant groups." Listen and repeat.

scholar<u>ship</u>   p<u>l</u>eased   cele<u>br</u>ate

b ▶10.13 Underline the consonant groups in the words below. Then practice saying the words. Listen and check.

dreams   brave   crazy   frightened   flight
agree   Africa   glasses   asleep   climate

c ▶10.14 Look at the words with three consonant sounds together (three sounds, but not always three letters). Listen and underline them.

asked   balanced   scream   sixth   text   strength
lamps   world   watched   spread

d Practice saying the words in 2b and 2c that are difficult for you.

3 LISTENING

a In Part 2, Ruby said, "There's something else we have to celebrate." What do you think she'll say next?

b ▶10.15 Listen to Part 3 and check. They celebrate four things altogether. What are they?

c Which person ... ?

1 tells them to celebrate the scholarship
2 cuts the cake
3 thinks they should have a party
4 announces the date for the party
5 looks relaxed

4 USEFUL LANGUAGE
Describing how you felt

a ▶ 10.16 Complete what Maya says with the words in the box. Then listen and check.

get believe can't surprised so over couldn't

I _____ _____ it. I was _____ _____. A scholarship!
I still _____ _____ _____ it.

b 💬 Discuss the questions.

1 How does Maya say she felt?
   a) happy   b) disappointed   c) surprised
2 Which word has the main stress in each sentence? Practice saying the sentences.

c Here are some more ways to describe how you felt.

1 ☐ I wasn't expecting it.   3 ☐ I was really pleased.
2 ☐ It was quite a blow.   4 ☐ I was expecting it.

Which means ... ?

a I was surprised   c I was happy
b I wasn't surprised   d I was shocked or disappointed

d Choose one of the situations below. Take notes to describe how you felt and why, but don't mention what happened. Use expressions in 4a and 4c.

1 Your boss called you into his office and said that you were fired.
2 You just won $10,000 on the lottery.
3 You didn't prepare for a test and you failed it.
4 Your best friend told you he/she is getting married.
5 Someone stole your wallet.
6 You were promoted.

e 💬 Read your sentences aloud. Can other students guess the situation?

I wasn't expecting it.

I was so surprised because I only bought one ticket.

I still can't believe it.

I was really pleased.

It was quite a blow.

I really can't get over it.

5 CONVERSATION SKILLS
Interrupting and announcing news

a ▶ 10.15 Listen to Part 3 again. Complete the remarks.

1 Hold _____.
2 There's something _____ we have to celebrate.
3 _____ me, but can we eat this cake _____?
4 Just a _____.
5 There's one more _____.

b Which remarks ... ?

1 are ways to stop a conversation from ending
2 are ways to show you are about to say something important

c Answer these questions.

1 At the end of each remark, does the voice ... ?
   a stay high
   b go down
2 Does this show the other person ... ?
   a that you've finished speaking
   b that you haven't finished speaking

d Practice saying the remarks.

6 SPEAKING

a Work in groups of four (A, B, C, and D). You're in a restaurant. You each have an important piece of news to tell your group.

Student A: You've just been offered a new job.
Student B: You've won a free trip to Lima for two weeks.
Student C: You're getting married.
Student D: You've won a prize in a poetry competition.

Work alone and decide:
- what details you will give
- which expressions you will use in 4a, 4c, and 5a.

b 💬 Have a conversation. Take turns announcing your news. Then continue talking until the next person interrupts.

✓ UNIT PROGRESS TEST

→ CHECK YOUR PROGRESS

You can now do the Unit Progress Test.

10D | SKILLS FOR WRITING
I forced myself to be calm

1 SPEAKING AND LISTENING

a 💬📱 Discuss the questions.

1 Have you ever performed activities like these in public? If so, what was it like? If not, how do you think it would feel?
2 What preparation is required to perform in public?
3 What do you think it takes to be successful in these activities?

b ▶ 10.17 Listen to Rosa speak to her teacher Kurt and answer the questions.

1 What is Rosa learning to play?
2 What's her ambition?
3 Does Kurt mention any of the ideas you discussed in 1a?

c ▶ 10.17 Listen again and take notes about the following topics.

1 Rosa's level of motivation
2 the three choices Kurt outlines
3 the way he suggests she could deal with pressure

d 💬📱 Discuss the questions.

1 What do you think Rosa should do? Give reasons for your answer.
2 Do you know of someone who has tried to excel in a demanding activity or job? What was their experience?
3 Do you think the sacrifices these people often need to make are worth it? Why / Why not?

Rosa and Kurt

ROSA'S DIARY

THE ULTIMATE GOAL

I sat in the dressing room and sighed. The moment had arrived. After months of hard practice, I was about to go on stage and perform in my first major competition. I looked at myself in the mirror. I looked like I could be a classical music pianist, but did I feel like one? There was a difference between the image I saw and what I felt when I closed my eyes.

I put my hands on my knees, breathing slowly to calm down. I repeated everything Kurt had told me, "You've practiced, you are well-prepared, and you can do this." But the thought that I would soon have to play for such a large audience was unnerving.

There was a knock at the door. It was the stage manager. Time for me to go on stage. I left the dressing room, feeling the butterflies in my stomach beat more insistently. I walked along the corridor to the steps that led to the wings of the stage. As we walked slowly up the stairs, the stage manager wished me good luck. "Can luck help me now?" I asked myself.

I stood in the wings, staring at the floor of the stage. I could hear the murmur of the audience – a wall of sound standing between me and the music. "Ladies and gentlemen," said the announcer. The murmur dissolved and there was quiet. My name was announced, and I stepped into a flood of light.

I took one step and was almost blinded by the stage lights. Where is the piano? I can't see anything! My heart was racing. But we had practiced this at the rehearsal yesterday. You know the way. You know where to go and what you have to do.

I began to cross the space between the wings of the stage and the piano stool. The audience applauded, and this wave of sound seemed to draw me across the stage. I tried to smile, but I'm not sure if I did. I eventually reached the piano and remembered to bow to the audience. I slowly took my seat on the stool, trying to keep my breathing regular. I forced myself to be calm. Silence. A moment of complete concentration.

I raise my hands and they float above the piano keys. I feel the adrenaline running through my body. Remember the final words of advice: go with the music, don't worry about mistakes, and stay in the moment, stay in the music.

My fingers touch the piano keys and I begin to play. I still feel the adrenaline, but it's working for me. Everything is falling into place. The notes float from my hands, and the warmth of the audience embraces me.

That was the very first time I performed in the competition. A week later, I returned for the finals and played with the state orchestra. And I won the competition! I've also been accepted by the Juilliard School of Music. It might feel like I've made it. But, in reality, I know that I've only started.

2 READING

a Read an excerpt from "Rosa's Diary" and answer the questions.

1 What event does Rosa describe?
2 What is the dominant feeling?
3 What is the outcome?

b Read the diary again. Take notes on Rosa's thoughts, feelings, and sensations at each of the following steps.

1 in the dressing room
2 from the dressing room to the wings
3 in the wings
4 moving across the stage
5 sitting at the piano

c 💬 Tell your partner about a time you had to do something that made you feel nervous.

3 WRITING SKILLS
Making a story interesting

a The writer uses various ways to make the story interesting. Find one more example of these in the story.

1 short sentences to describe Rosa's thoughts and feelings
   The moment had arrived.
2 questions to show what she was thinking
   … but did I feel like one?
3 phrases with verb + *-ing* to describe actions and events
   I put my hands on my knees, breathing slowly to calm down.

b Match the beginnings in A to the endings in B to make more sentences from "first time" stories.

A
1 ☐ She dove into the water,
2 ☐ He stood up in front of the meeting,
3 ☐ She couldn't stop tuning the guitar,
4 ☐ He walked on to the soccer field,
5 ☐ She peered into the microscope,

B
a looking down and pretending the crowd wasn't there.
b playing nervously with his slide clicker.
c hoping she'd be able to see more of the sample.
d breathing in deeply before she hit.
e humming the first few notes of the song repeatedly.

c Choose one of the beginnings in A. Continue the story, using a new phrase with verb + *-ing*.

d 💬 Switch stories with a partner. Continue their story by adding a sentence of your own. Read the story back to your partner.

e Look at these examples. What verb tenses does the writer use?

I repeated to myself everything Kurt had told me …
My heart was racing. But we had practiced this at the rehearsal yesterday.

Which tense does the writer use … ?

1 to tell the main events of the story
2 to refer to an earlier event that explains what happened

f Continue these sentences with your own ideas, using the past perfect tense.

1 When I opened the PowerPoint presentation on my laptop, all the slides were blank.
2 I opened my mouth to sing, but the microphone wasn't working.
3 When I hit the ball, it went sailing up into the crowd.
4 As I stepped on to the ice, I realized I wasn't wearing gloves.

4 WRITING

a Take notes about the first time you did something. It can be the same situation you talked about in 2c or a different situation. Use these ideas to help.

- where the event took place
- preparation for the event
- different steps you had to go through
- your feelings before and during the event
- any problems/obstacles you encountered
- the outcome

b Write your story. Remember to use …

- short sentences
- direct questions
- verb + *-ing*
- past perfect to explain the background actions.

c Read other students' stories.

1 Did they use all the writing skills suggested in 4b?
2 Which story was … ?
   - the most unusual
   - the greatest challenge
   - the most nerve-wracking
   - the most amusing

UNIT 10
Review and extension

1 GRAMMAR

a Complete the conversation using the verbs in parentheses with a past modal of deduction.

A Who left those flowers for us?
B It ^{1}_____ (be) Rachel – she's out of town at the moment.
A Janet ^{2}_____ (leave) them – she occasionally surprises us like that.
B Actually, it ^{3}_____ (be) Elaine. She called this morning and said something about a surprise for us.
A Well, whoever left them – they're beautiful.

b Imagine different past possibilities for the following situations. Take notes.

1 You check your online bank account and find someone has deposited $100 into the account.
2 You arrive home and find the front door wide open.
3 You receive a package addressed to you containing a brand-new tablet and an anonymous card saying, "Enjoy!"

c 💬 Discuss your different ideas.

d Put the verbs in parentheses in the correct form.

1 My business degree wasn't very interesting or useful when it came to finding a job. I wish I _____ (study) history in college instead.
2 She didn't start studying Mandarin until she went to China. She should _____ (take) a class about six months before going there.
3 In his new job, he has to interpret a lot of statistics. If only he _____ (pay) more attention in math classes in high school.

2 VOCABULARY

a Correct the adjective prefixes.

1 She's very good with young children, but she can get a little inpatient with teenagers.
2 He left without saying goodbye – that's very unpolite.
3 They made an inexpected visit to the children's hospital. It was a nice surprise for the patients.
4 We were extremely missatisfied with the level of service we experienced during our stay.

b Complete the sentences using the correct verbs in the box.

work	overcome	cope	tackle

1 When I lived in Veracruz, I found it easy to _____ with the heat.
2 On Sundays, I like nothing more than to _____ a really difficult crossword puzzle.
3 He managed to _____ his shyness and make friends in college.
4 My grammar's pretty good – I just need to _____ on my pronunciation.

3 WORDPOWER way

a Match the *way* expression in 1–6 with the correct meanings in a–f.

1 ☐ I'm sorry, but there's *no way* I can sign that contract – the conditions aren't clearly described.
2 ☐ *One way or another,* we have to know all that vocabulary for the test.
3 ☐ I thought it would be cheaper to go by bus than train, but it was *the other way around.*
4 ☐ After a quick dinner, we *made our way* to the concert.
5 ☐ I ran *all the way* around the park, and I'm exhausted.
6 ☐ *In some ways,* it would be easier to not go abroad on vacation this year.

a We can't avoid it.
b I can't do it.
c We went there.
d It's partly true.
e I went the complete distance.
f It was the opposite.

b Replace the incorrect *way* expressions. Check (✓) the ones that are correct.

1 ☐ We traveled in some ways to the end of the island.
2 ☐ I thought she'd be nicer than her brother, but it was one way or another.
3 ☐ I don't feel well and there's no way I can go out.
4 ☐ All the way, it might be easier to talk to him than send an email.
5 ☐ If you hear an alarm, please make your way toward the exit as quickly as possible.

c Answer the questions. Take notes.

1 What's something that you would never do?
2 When did you last go the whole distance somewhere?
3 What's something you think is partly true?
4 What's a situation where you found that the opposite was true?

d 💬 Discuss the situations in 3c. Use a *way* expression with each example.

🔄 REVIEW YOUR PROGRESS

How well did you do in this unit? Write 3, 2, or 1 for each objective.
3 = very well   2 = well   1 = not so well

I CAN ...	
speculate about the past	☐
discuss life achievements	☐
describe how I felt	☐
write a narrative.	☐

126

This page is intentionally left blank.

6B PAIR A

a Prepare for a discussion. You believe that everything in the world changes and languages naturally die out. There's no point in trying to stop that from happening, and it doesn't really matter.

Use these arguments or prepare your own:
- In the modern world, everyone needs to speak a major world language.
- A lot of tribal languages are not adapted to modern life. They belong to a way of life that is dying.
- If young people speak a major language, they can travel and get jobs.
- Languages die because young people don't want to speak them. It's wrong to try to force them.

b ≫ Now go back to p. 73.

9C STUDENT A

a 💬 Have two conversations.

> **Conversation 1**
> Tell your partner you have a surprise for them to do with entertainment. Make them try and guess. Eventually tell them it's free tickets for them to go and see *Hamlet*. If your partner looks a little disappointed, check that they like the theater – you're sure they told you they did.

> **Conversation 2**
> Your partner has a surprise for you to do with a sports game. Try to find out what it is. You like going to tennis matches and soccer games, but you don't really like basketball. Try to be polite and grateful.

b ≫ Now go to p. 112.

10A STUDENT A

a Read the story.

> **Separated Twin Boys with Almost Identical Lives**
>
> Stories of identical twins are often incredible, but perhaps none more so than those of identical twin boys born in Ohio. They were separated at birth and grew up in different families. Unknown to each other, both families named them James.
> The boys grew up not even knowing each other, but they both became police officers and both married women named Linda. They both had sons, who one named James Alan and the other named James Allan. They both got divorced and then married again to women named Betty. They both owned dogs they named Toy. They met for the first time after 45 years.

b ≫ Now go back to p. 118.

7C STUDENT A

a Imagine what you would do with the room shown in the picture. Think about:
- how you could use different parts of it (e.g., sleeping, working, watching TV)
- what furniture you might put in it
- where you could put different items (e.g., pictures, a TV, a computer).

b Draw a rough plan of the room to show what you would do. Think how you could use:
- expressions for imagining from 4a on p. 87.
- vague phrases from 5a and 5d on p. 87.

c 💬 Show Student B your plan and tell him/her how you imagine the room. Then listen to Student B and ask questions about his/her room.

d ≫ Now go back to p. 87.

8B PAIR B

a Read the story and answer the questions.
1 Why was the art teacher given the job?
2 What was wrong with his résumé?
3 Why did the principal fire him?

The Art Teacher

A school was looking for a new art teacher. They had received several applications, including one from a well-known local artist who also had many years' teaching experience. He made a good impression in the interview, so they offered him the job.

On his résumé, he had listed an MA in art history. After the school employed him, they discovered that he had started an MA course but never finished it. His résumé was clearly wrong.

The principal called him into her office and asked him about it. He explained that he hadn't finished the MA because he'd had to spend a year in the army. He had intended to write "Course work completed for MA" – it was just a simple mistake.

The principal of the school was faced with a difficult decision. She didn't believe the art teacher, but he had already started working and he was doing a good job. However, after thinking it over, she decided to fire him.

b What do you think the principal should have done? What would you have done?

c ≫ Now go back to p. 96.

8B

The researchers expected employees to be more likely to contact the wallet's "owner" if it contained no cash, but might keep the wallets that did contain cash. They were surprised to find that the opposite happened. People were more likely to return the wallet when it contained more money: 71% of the wallets with the most cash were returned, 51% of those with a small amount of cash, and 40% of the wallets without cash. Also, people returned all the money and didn't keep any for themselves. Fear of being found out didn't seem to be a factor, as it made no difference whether or not there were surveillance cameras.

The researchers suggest two explanations for this. One is that we care about people losing things, and the more money they have lost, the more we care. But another explanation is that people don't want to see themselves as a thief, and the more money there is in the wallet, the more it would "feel like stealing" if they didn't return it.

So it seems that people are more honest worldwide than you might think, and also that they care more about each other than you might expect.

≫ Now go back to p. 95.

9C STUDENT B

a 💬🗨 Have two conversations.

Conversation 1
Student A is going to draw a picture in four steps. After each step use expressions in 2c (p.110) to show that you're unsure what the picture is. Get Student A to explain or add more detail to the picture until you can guess what it is.

Conversation 2
Look at the guide to drawing a penguin. Follow the steps to draw your own penguin. Student A will try and guess what you are drawing. Be prepared to explain or add more detail.

What in the world is that?

I don't have a clue what that is.

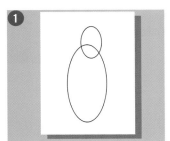

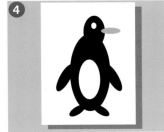

b ≫ Now go back to p. 110.

9C STUDENT B

a 💬🗨 Have two conversations.

Conversation 1
Your partner has a surprise for you. Try to find out what it is. You like going to classical music concerts and the opera, but you're not very interested in theater events. Try to be polite and grateful.

Conversation 2
Tell your partner you have a surprise for them to do with a sports game. Make them try and guess. Eventually tell them it's free tickets for them to go to a basketball game. If your partner looks a little disappointed, check that they like basketball – you're sure they told you they did.

b ≫ Now go to p. 112.

7B

a This is a picture from a reality TV show. Talk about the questions. What do you think?

- Is the woman really suffering or is she acting?
- Would you like to be in her situation? Why / Why not?

b ≫ Now go back to p. 83.

9A STUDENT B

a 💬🗨 Describe your invention to Student A, but don't tell him/her what it is. Ask him/her to guess what the invention is. Use these expressions to help you.

This thing's made of …
You can hold it in your hand.
You can put it …
You can put something in it.
You can maybe find one in …
It might be useful after / when …

Portable Oxygen Booster
This portable oxygen booster increases available oxygen from 20% or lower up to 30%. You can use this in the office, while exercising, or anywhere you feel the need for a little extra air.

Ultraviolet Sterilizer

This is an ultraviolet sterilizer that can keep you from getting sick. You can use it to sterilize everyday things from computer keyboards to kitchen items and even beds. It uses ultraviolet radiation to kill bacteria. It's ideal for any home.

b ≫ Now go back to p. 106.

a 💬 Describe your invention to Student B, but don't tell him/her what it is. Ask him/her to guess what the invention is. Use these expressions to help you.

You can hold it in your hand.
You can put it …
You can put something in it.
You can maybe find one in …
It might be useful after/when …

Anti-Snoring Pillow

This pillow uses a sensor to detect snoring and then responds by vibrating. Tests show that this is efficient in reducing snoring. In addition, the pillow has an internal recording device that allows you to record your snoring and monitor the effectiveness of the pillow.

Ear Dryer

You can use this to dry the inside of your ear after you've had a shower, bath, or swim. You place the device in your ear and it blows hot air. The makers suggest you use it after you have dried your ears with a towel.

b ≫ Now go back to p. 106.

7C STUDENT B

a Imagine what you would do with the room shown in the picture. Think about:
- how you could use different parts of it (e.g., sleeping, working, watching TV)
- what furniture you might put in it
- where you could put different items (e.g., pictures, a TV, a computer).

b Draw a rough plan of the room to show what you would do. Think how you could use:
- expressions for imagining from 4a on p. 87.
- vague phrases from 5a and 5d on p. 87.

c 💬 Listen to Student A and ask questions about his/her room. Then show Student A your plan and tell him/her how you imagine your room.

d ≫ Now go back to p. 87.

---

a Read the final part of the story about Barry Minkow.

While he was in prison, Barry Minkow became a new person (or so it seemed.) He trained as a pastor and he wrote a book about his life, with the profits going to the people he owed money to. He was released from prison after only seven years.

After coming out of prison, Barry Minkow worked as a pastor. He also gave talks in schools about the mistakes he had made. He became well-known as a fraud expert, often appearing on TV, and he set up a company which investigated company fraud. At the time, very few people questioned whether he was really the reformed character that he claimed to be. It later turned out that he was making huge amounts of money from buying and selling shares in the companies he was "investigating." He was sentenced to five more years in prison.

While he was a pastor, he was very good at persuading people to donate money to the church, but after a while, some people began to wonder where their money was really going. Later, investigations showed that he had opened false bank accounts and tricked people into making donations to the church, which had actually gone into his own pocket. He was sentenced to five more years in prison for stealing more than $3 million from church members.

b ≫ Now go back to p. 107.

6A STUDENT B

a Read about the two tourist destinations. Take notes about them. Think about which you prefer and why.

b 💬 Tell Student A about the destination you prefer. Try to agree on which of your two destinations to visit. Use your notes from **a** to persuade your partner to visit your place.

HAMPI

This small village in South West India offers the chance to discover a whole new culture. Until 500 years ago, it was the capital of the Vijayanagara Empire. There's an incredible number of monuments and ruins that belonged to this ancient civilization. Perhaps the most impressive is the Virupaksha Temple. Hampi is a cultural experience like no other.

Rotorua

This small city in New Zealand is surrounded by a series of stunningly beautiful lakes and forests. But what makes it so special is all its geothermal activity. You can see hot steam shoot from the ground in the form of a geyser, while nearby a pool of mud boils away. Rotorua is dramatic and unique – it's definitely worth a visit.

c ≫ Now go back to p. 70.

9C STUDENT A

a 💬🗣 Have two conversations.

> **Conversation 1**
> Look at the guide to drawing a panda. Follow the steps to draw your own panda. Student B will try to guess what you are drawing. Be prepared to explain or add more details.

> **Conversation 2**
> Student B is going to draw a picture in four steps. After each step, use expressions in 2c (p.110) to show that you're unsure what the picture is. Get Student B to explain or add more details to the picture until you can guess what it is.

What in the world is that?

I don't have a clue what that is.

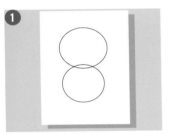

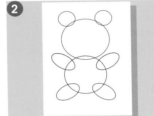

b ⟫ Now go back to p. 110.

6B PAIR B

a Prepare for a discussion. You believe that it's important to keep languages from dying out. Every time we lose a language, we lose part of our culture.

Use these arguments or prepare your own:
- There's no reason why people shouldn't speak several languages: their own language and one or two "bigger" languages.
- Languages die out because people feel ashamed of them. It's important to educate people to respect and value minor languages.
- The world needs variety – the world would be very boring if people all spoke one language.
- Many tribal languages contain knowledge about plants, medicines, and the environment that could be very useful. We need to preserve this knowledge.

b ⟫ Now go back to p. 73.

6A STUDENT A

a Read about the two tourist destinations. Take notes about them. Think about which you prefer and why.

b 💬🗣 Tell Student B about the destination you prefer. Try to agree on which of your two destinations to visit. Use your notes from **a** to persuade your partner to visit your place.

Dominica
A small but beautiful Caribbean island with superb beaches and tropical rainforests filled with exotic bird life. Dominica's biggest attraction is a boiling lake. After a three-hour trek through a stunningly beautiful forest, you come to a lake that is hot and steaming. No one knows about it yet, so go there before everyone else does!

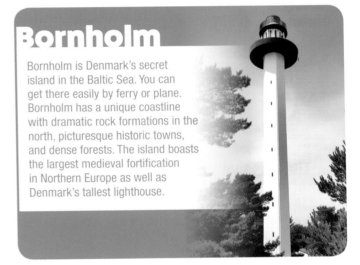

Bornholm
Bornholm is Denmark's secret island in the Baltic Sea. You can get there easily by ferry or plane. Bornholm has a unique coastline with dramatic rock formations in the north, picturesque historic towns, and dense forests. The island boasts the largest medieval fortification in Northern Europe as well as Denmark's tallest lighthouse.

⟫ Now go back to p. 70.

10A STUDENT B

a Read the story.

> **A Falling Boy Caught Twice by the Same Man**
> In Detroit, sometime in the 1930s, a baby fell from a window. But it fell onto a passerby, a man named Joseph Figlock. He broke the baby's fall, and it survived unharmed.
> A year later, the same baby fell from the same window again. Once again, Joseph Figlock happened to be passing by. The baby fell on him again, and the same thing happened!

b ⟫ Now go back to p. 118.

6A Gerunds and infinitives

▶ 06.03 **verb + -ing**

When verb + -ing functions like a noun it is called a gerund. We use gerunds:

- when a verb is (part of) the subject of a sentence:
  Swimming is good for you. / **Meeting** you last week was a real pleasure.
- after prepositions (e.g., about, by, without, of, etc.):
  I worry too much **about making** mistakes.
  They escaped **by digging** a tunnel under the wall.

▶ 06.04 **infinitive**

We use infinitives:

- after adjectives (e.g., happy, pleased, easy, difficult, dangerous, safe, possible):
  It's **easy to find** your way into the city center, but it's very **difficult to get** out again.
- to express purpose (= what a person wants to achieve):
  We're going to the beach **to lie** in the sun. (= because we want to lie in the sun)
  To watch the clip again, click "replay." (= if you want to watch it again)

> **Tip** Be careful with verb forms after to. The word to is sometimes a preposition and sometimes part of the infinitive.
> I'm looking forward **to seeing** you.
> I hope **to see** you. (NOT ~~I hope to seeing~~)

▶ 06.05 **verb + verb**

There are many verbs that are followed by gerunds (e.g., I **enjoy painting**) and many that are followed by infinitives (e.g., I **want to watch**). There are also a few that allow both patterns with a change of meaning:

- try + infinitive: I **tried to talk** to him, but he didn't answer his phone. (= I attempted to do it)
- try + gerund: I **tried talking** to him, but he's still angry. (= I did it but it didn't work)
- remember + infinitive: Please **remember to buy** some milk. (= a job for the future)
- remember + gerund: I **remember hearing** that song for the first time. (= an experience in the past)
- go on + infinitive: After explaining the theory, I'll **go on to describe** some examples. (= stop one thing and start the next)
- keep + gerund: The professor **kept talking** for over an hour. (= didn't stop)

> **Tip** stop can be followed by a gerund or an infinitive of purpose:
> I **stopped drinking** coffee. (= I don't drink it now)
> I **stopped to drink** coffee. (= I stopped because I wanted to drink coffee in a café)

▶ 06.06 **Sense verbs**

Verbs connected with senses can be followed by an object and verb + -ing. (e.g., look at / see / watch / notice / observe / hear / listen to / feel / smell / taste):

I **watched** the people **walking** around.
I could **smell** something **burning**.

6B The passive

▶ 06.14 We can use the passive:

- when we don't know who did something / what caused something, or when this is not important.
  These words **were written** thousands of years ago.
- when the agent (the doer) is very obvious.
  Which languages **are spoken** in your family?
- when the main thing we are talking about is the object of the verb.
  I read a really interesting article today. It **was written** by someone who spent a year living in a jungle. (It = the article)

The passive is formed with the verb be in the appropriate tense + past participle.

	Active	Passive
Simple present	They **use** it.	It **is used**.
Simple past	They **used** it.	It **was used**.
Present continuous	They **are using** it.	It **is being used**.
Past continuous	They **were using** it.	It **was being used**.
Present perfect	They **have used** it.	It **has been used**.
Past perfect	They **had used** it.	It **had been used**.
Future	They **will use** it.	It **will be used**.
	They **are going to use** it.	It **is going to be used**.
Base form (e.g., after modal verbs)	They **can use** it.	It **can be used**.
	They **might use** it.	It **might be used**.

▶ 06.15 **Prepositions after made**

We can use a range of prepositions after passives with made:

- Made + by + method: These cakes are **made by hand / by mixing** cornflakes with chocolate.
- Made + with + tool: I think these marks were **made with a knife**.
- Made + of + material: The wings are **made of very strong plastic**.
- Made + from / out of + original object: Our table is **made from / out of an old door**.

Our table **is made from / out of** an old door.

6A Gerunds and infinitives

a <u>Underline</u> the correct verb forms.

1 I was looking forward to *hear* / <u>*hearing*</u> your ideas.
2 We need to make an appointment to *see* / *seeing* them again.
3 I'm still getting used to *be* / *being* a manager.
4 Riding an elephant is similar to *ride* / *riding* a horse.
5 He doesn't find it easy to *talk* / *talking* to anyone.

b Match the sentence halves.

1 ☐ Why don't you try …
2 ☐ We're going to try …
3 ☐ Can you please stop …
4 ☐ You'll have to stop …
5 ☐ Did you remember …
6 ☐ I don't remember …
7 ☐ Start with the easy questions and then go on …
8 ☐ We started in the morning and kept …

a … to win the game. It'll be hard, but we still have a chance.
b … to turn off the lights before you went out?
c … playing until it was dark.
d … to buy some gas. You're going to run out soon.
e … restarting the computer? That usually works for me.
f … to try the ones that are left.
g … making that noise? I can't concentrate.
h … buying these shoes. Are you sure they're mine?

c Complete the sentences with the correct form of the verbs in parentheses.

1 I'll be happy <u>to help</u> (help) you find somewhere to stay.
2 He spent two years without _____ (speak) to another person.
3 _____ (live) in another country is the easiest way of _____ (learn) a foreign language.
4 Can I borrow your laptop _____ (check) my emails?
5 Suddenly, I noticed a young man _____ (run) toward me.
6 I'm afraid of _____ (be) alone in the dark.
7 _____ (avoid) the risk of misunderstandings, I'll explain everything twice.
8 Would it be possible _____ (leave) five minutes early?
9 _____ (spend) a year as a volunteer teacher was one of the best experiences of my life.
10 As he waited for his results, he could feel his heart _____ (beat) in his chest.

d ≫ Now go back to p. 69.

6B The passive

a Complete the sentences with the correct passive form of the verb in parentheses.

1 The local people are angry because these old trees <u>are going to be cut</u> (cut) down next week.
2 The first email between two organizations _____ (send) in 1971.
3 Currently, English _____ (use) as an official language in almost 60 countries.
4 I promise that you _____ (inform) as soon as your bags arrive.
5 The thief _____ (not / catch) yet, but I'm sure they'll catch him soon.
6 By the time we arrived, all the best seats _____ (already / take), so we had to sit all the way in the back.

b Rewrite the sentences in the passive.

1 I wrote that report.
2 My sister told us about this restaurant.
3 We can only dream of the technology of 2100.
4 Someone had already built this bridge 1,000 years ago.
5 You can't always depend on Martina.
6 I'm sure they'll look after you well.

That report _____ <u>was written by me</u> _____.
We _____.
The technology of 2100 _____.
This bridge _____.
Martina _____.
I'm sure you _____.

c Complete the sentences with the correct prepositions.

1 Jam is made <u>out of / from</u> fruit.
2 This toy car was made _____ an old shoe box.
3 I can't believe this music was made _____ a computer.
4 If you want a perfect paper airplane, it must be made _____ scissors and glue.
5 Windows in a plane are made _____ special glass, so they don't break easily.
6 All our clothes are made _____ local wool and _____ local people.

d ≫ Now go back to p. 73.

7A *too / enough*; so / *such*

It's **such** a beautiful city, but there are **too** many people! It's **such** a shame!

▶ 07.01 *too* and *enough*

We use *too* and *not enough* to explain problems, when something is more than the right amount or less than the right amount:

*Oh, no! There are **too** many people and there is**n't enough** food! What's everybody going to eat?*

We often use *enough* to tell somebody not to worry:

*Don't worry. We have **enough** food. I bought a lot of food this morning.*

We use adjective + *enough* and *enough* + noun:

	More than the right amount	The right amount	Less than the right amount
With adjectives	*It's **too** warm to play tennis.*	*It's warm **enough** to go to the beach.*	*It is**n't** warm **enough** to have a picnic.*
With count nouns	*There are **too many** people. I can't see anything.*	*There are **enough** people for a game of volleyball.*	*There are**n't enough** people for a game of soccer.*
With noncount nouns	*I spend **too much** time in Internet chat rooms.*	*I have **enough** time to bake a cake.*	*There is**n't enough** time to go shopping.*

▶ 07.02

💬 **Tip** After *too* and *enough*, we often use *to* + infinitive:

*It's **too** late **to walk** home, but I don't have **enough** money **to pay** for a taxi.*

▶ 07.03 *so / such*

We use *so* and *such* to draw attention to the extreme quality of something. We can use *so* before an adjective and *such* before adjective + noun.

- *so* + adjective: *Why are you **so happy?*** (= why are you as happy as you are?)
- *such* + *a/an* + adjective + singular noun: *It's **such a beautiful day!*** (= it's a very beautiful day)
- *such* + adjective + plural noun: *They're **such friendly people!***

💬 **Tip** We can use *such a* + noun to express a positive or negative opinion:

*It's **such a pity / shame** you missed the beginning!* (= I'm so sorry / sad.)
*You're **such a genius**! (= You're so smart!)*
*The meal was **such a waste** of money!*
*It's always **such a pleasure** to talk to you.*

▶ 07.04

After *so / such*, we often use a *that* clause:

*It was **such** a nice place **that** we decided to stay another week.* (= we decided to stay because it was extremely nice)
*I ate **so** much food **that** I felt sick.*

7B Causative *have / get*

We use the structure *have / get* + object + past participle to talk about things that we arrange or pay for but don't actually do ourselves. *Have* is slightly more formal than *get*.

▶ 07.08

	have / get	Object	Past participle
They're	*having*	*their kitchen*	*painted.*
When are you going to	*get*	*your hair*	*cut?*
I	*had*	*my car*	*fixed.*
She wants to	*have*	*her book*	*published.*

We can mention the agent (the person who did the action) after *by*:
*She had her dress made **by a top designer**.*

▶ 07.09

💬 **Tip** We use a reflexive pronoun (e.g., *myself, herself, ourselves*) to emphasize that we **didn't** arrange or pay for somebody else to do something:

*I wanted to get my pants shortened, but it was too expensive, so I did it **myself**.*

We can use the structure *have* + something + past participle to talk about experiences that are caused by other people. These experiences are usually negative:

*He **had his phone stolen**.* (= He experienced the situation where somebody stole his phone.)

We can use the structure *get* + something + past participle to focus on the end results of an activity rather than the activity itself:

*I don't care how you do it – just **get this work done**!*
(= finish it or pay for somebody to finish it)

I wanted to **get** my pants **shortened,** but it was too expensive, so I did it myself.

7A *too / enough; so / such*

a Complete the sentences with words in the box. Use each word or phrase twice.

| enough   too   too many   too much |

1 She speaks pretty quickly but she makes _too many_ mistakes.
2 Oh, no! We don't have _____ milk. Can you go to the store and buy some?
3 They're nice children, but they make _____ noise.
4 We wanted to go out, but it was _____ cold.
5 They spend _____ time watching TV. It's not healthy!
6 Your project isn't perfect, but it's good _____.
  You don't need to do it again.
7 You should take a bus – it's _____ far to walk.
8 _____ people attended the meeting. Everyone was talking at the same time and they couldn't make any decisions.

b Match the sentence halves.

1 ☐ They're so …
2 ☐ It was such a …
3 ☐ You've read that book so many …
4 ☐ She wrote her complaint in such a …
5 ☐ There was so much …
6 ☐ They're such …

a … times that you must know every word by now.
b … way that we thought she was being kind.
c … nice people that I'm sure you'll like them!
d … boring movie that we left halfway through.
e … lazy that they never do any homework.
f … food that we couldn't eat it all.

c Rewrite the second sentence so that it means the same as the first. Use the words in parentheses and *so*, *such*, *too*, or *enough*.

1 They went by plane because they're rich. (that)
  They're _so rich that_ they went by plane.
2 I'm so sorry that we didn't see you. (pity)
  It's _____ that we didn't see you.
3 He's too young to be a doctor. (old)
  He isn't _____ be a doctor.
4 I didn't go out because I was so tired. (too)
  I was _____ go out.
5 That player's so good that he plays for his national team. (such)
  He's _____ he plays for his national team.
6 It was such a serious situation that they had to call the police. (so)
  The situation _____ they had to call the police.

d ⟫ Now go back to p. 81.

7B Causative *have / get*

a Match the sentences with reasons A–C for using causative *have / get*.

1 ☐ Did you get your hair done? It looks lovely.
2 ☐ My boss isn't very good at getting his team motivated.
3 ☐ I've had my heart broken too many times – I don't want to fall in love again.
4 ☐ I need to get my eyes checked. I can't see very well.
5 ☐ My neighbors had their car stolen last week.
6 ☐ I just want to get this work done quickly so I can relax again.
7 ☐ I had my portrait painted by a wonderful artist.
8 ☐ Last time I went to the dentist, I had to have two teeth taken out.

A The subject arranges or pays for somebody to do something.

B The subject has a bad experience caused by someone else.

C The speaker focuses on the end result rather than the activity itself.

b Rewrite the phrases in **bold** with causative *have / get*. Don't include the words in parentheses.

1 I'm going to (**pay sb) to clean my apartment.**
2 I'll (**arrange for sb) to install the new programs**.
3 Can you try to **finish the project** as quickly as possible?
4 (**sb) stole my email password** last week.
5 Robert, would you like to **start the meeting**?
6 We **really need to clean the apartment** – it's such a mess.

c ⟫ Now go back to p. 84.

8A Future real and present / future unreal conditionals

▶ 08.02 We can use both future real and present / future unreal conditionals to talk about future possibilities.

The future real conditional:
The future real conditional describes possible or likely future events and the expected results of those events:
if + simple present, *will* + infinitive
If I save a little every month, **I'll be able to afford** a new car soon.

The present / future unreal conditional:
We use the present / future unreal conditional to talk about imagined events or states and their consequences. They can be about the unreal present or unlikely future events:
if + simple past, *would* + infinitive
*if I **had** $1 for every time I've heard that, **I'd be** a millionaire.*
If I saved $50 every month, **I'd have** enough for a new computer by the end of the year.

> 💬 **Tip** We use the phrase *if I were you* to give advice:
> **If I were you**, **I wouldn't** borrow so much money.

> 💬 **Tip** We can use *going to* instead of *will* in future real conditional sentences: *If I see her tomorrow, I'm **going to tell** her my news.*

We often use other past / present tenses in the *if* clause:
*If you**'ve finished** your test and you**'re waiting** to leave, you **should come** to my desk.*

We can also use imperatives in the main clause:
*If you've finished your test and you're waiting to leave, please **come** to my desk.*

We can use modals other than *will* / *would* in the main clause (e.g., *might*, *could*, *should*, etc.):
*If I **weren't feeling** so tired, I **might** go for a run.*

If I **save** a little every month, I'll **be able** to afford a new car soon.

If I **had** $1 for every time, I've heard that, I'd **be** a millionaire.

8B Past unreal conditional; *should have* + past participle

▶ 08.05 *should have* + past participle
We can use the structure *should have* + past participle to criticize other people's past actions:
*You **shouldn't have told** them about the party. I wanted it to be a surprise.*

Past unreal conditional
We use the past unreal conditional to talk about imagined past events or states and their consequences:
If I'd arrived five minutes earlier, **I'd have seen** the robbery. (But I arrived after the robbery, so I didn't see it.)

if clause	Main clause
If + past perfect	*would* + *have* + past participle
If you hadn't told me the answer,	**I'd have checked** on the Internet.
If there had been more time,	we **wouldn't have had** to hurry.

> 💬 **Tip** Be careful with *'d*. It's short for *had* in the *if* clause but *would* in the main clause. *If I **'d** known earlier, I **'d** have told you.*

We can use past perfect continuous in the *if* clause. We can also use *might* or *could* in the main clause:
*It was a horrible accident. If I **hadn't been wearing** a helmet, I **might** have been very badly hurt.* (But I was wearing a helmet, so I wasn't badly hurt.)

▶ 08.06 **Mixed conditionals**
We combine clauses from the present and past unreal conditional to talk about past conditions with a result in the present, or present conditions with a result in the past.

if clause	Main clause
*If those burglars **hadn't damaged** that painting last year, …* [Past unreal conditional]	*… it **would be** worth a fortune now.* [Present unreal conditional]
*If I **didn't have** such a good relationship with my family, …* [Present unreal conditional]	*… I **would have left** the city years ago.* [Past unreal conditional]

8A Future real and present / future unreal conditionals

a Complete the sentences with a future real or a present / future unreal conditional.

1 [likely] Be careful with my phone! If you ___lose___ (lose) it, I ___'ll be___ (be) very angry.

2 [unlikely] If somebody ___spoke___ (speak) to me like that, I ___'d be___ (be) really angry.

3 [likely] It _____ (be) much cheaper if you _____ (come) by bus.

4 [likely] If you _____ (not spend) more money on advertising, your sales _____ (go) down.

5 [unlikely] I think you _____ (have) a great time if you _____ (study) abroad.

6 [likely] If Tony _____ (not finish) work soon, he _____ (not be) here on time.

7 [unreal] If you _____ (know) how to drive, I _____ (not have) to drive you everywhere.

8 [advice] If I _____ (be) you, I _____ (not say) anything about this to Ricky.

9 [likely] I'm sure they _____ (not be) angry if you _____ (tell) them the truth.

10 [unreal] She _____ (not have) a chance of getting that job if she _____ (not speak) English so well.

11 [likely] If it _____ (not rain) tomorrow morning, I _____ (walk) to work.

12 [advice] I _____ (not touch) that wire if I _____ (be) you.

b Look at the pictures. Write sentences using the prompts. Use the future real or present / future unreal conditional.

1 OK, so I promise ___I'll give you $ 1 if you wash my car.___
[give you $1 / wash / my car]

2 Sorry. _____
_____
[love / go dancing tonight / not / have / so much work]

3 _____
[if / I / you / buy / new shoes]

4 Watch out! _____
[if / fall / might/ hurt yourself]

5 Wow – just imagine! _____
_____
[if / we / find / that gold / rich]

6 Of course it's not working!
_____
[it / not / work / if / turn it on]

c ≫ Now go back to p. 93.

8B Past unreal conditional; *should have* + past participle

a Write sentences about each situation. Use the past unreal conditional with the past perfect or past perfect continuous in the *if* clause.

1 I didn't take the test because I didn't know about it.
I ___would have taken the test if I'd known about it.___

2 They went to the same university, so they met and fell in love.
If _____

3 It was raining so we took the subway.
If _____

4 We didn't buy the picture because it was so expensive.
We _____

5 You didn't hear the phone because you were listening to music.
You _____

6 My parents gave me some money, so I was able to buy a car.
If _____

b Write sentences about these situations using *should have* + past participle. Use the words in parentheses.

1 Oh, no, they're going to be late again. [leave home earlier]
___They should have left home earlier.___

2 The customer was really rude. [he / not speak to me like that]
_____

3 You've made the alarm go off! [not press that button]
_____

4 I had no idea it was your birthday. [you / tell me]
_____

5 That car drove through the red light. [it / stop]
_____

6 She failed her driving test. [she / take / more driving lessons]
_____

c Match the sentence halves.

1 ☐ If we'd had more time, …
2 ☐ I'm sure Walter would have lent you some money …
3 ☐ If you hadn't driven me home, …
4 ☐ They'd be a lot richer …
5 ☐ I wouldn't have bought so much food …
6 ☐ If Gloria wasn't so nice, …

a … if they'd sold their apartment when prices were still high.
b … I'd still be at the station now.
c … if you'd told me only four people were coming.
d … we wouldn't have invited her to stay with us.
e … we'd have done more sightseeing.
f … if you'd asked him.

d ≫ Now go back to p. 96.

9A Relative clauses

> Did you know they've invented a car **that** keeps people from crashing?

▶ 09.04 Defining relative clauses

Defining relative clauses give essential information about a noun.

They've invented a car. **The car** keeps people from crashing.
*They've invented a car **that** keeps people from crashing!*

- *who* describes a person, and *which* describes a thing. In defining relative clauses, you can use *that* instead of both *who* and *which*:
  *This is the work **which** / **that** has to be finished today.*
  *The man **who** / **that** I needed to talk to wasn't available.*

When *who* / *which* / *that* replace **the object** of the clause, we can omit the relative pronoun:
*You're applying for **the job** (= object)*
*What's the job (**which** / **that**) you're applying for?*

- *where* describes a place:
  *There's a new shop in town **where** you can buy furniture.*
- *whose* describes possession:
  *The woman **whose apartment** was burglarized is named Mrs. Plater.*
- *when* describes times (e.g., *day* / *year* / *time*):
  *The days **when** I have to pick up the children are stressful.*

We sometimes use *who*, *which*, and *that* with prepositions. The prepositions usually come at the end of the sentence:
*There is a place nearby **which** / **that** we can stop at.*

▶ 09.05 Non-defining relative clauses

Non-defining relative clauses give extra information about a noun. The clause is not necessary for the sentence to make sense. A non-defining clause has a comma before it and either another comma, or a period after it:
*My new doctor, **who I had my first appointment with on Thursday**, recommended the medicine to me.*

In non-defining clauses, *which* can relate to a single noun or to the whole main clause:
*I'm going to Thailand next week, **which** is very exciting.*

There are two main differences between defining and non-defining clauses.

- we cannot use *that* in a non-defining clause:
  *Revolutionary technology, **which** is rare, usually requires a huge investment to develop.* NOT *Revolutionary technology, that is rare…*
- we can never omit the relative pronoun in a non-defining clause:
  *Jane, **who** I have always trusted, was the only person I told about the situation.* NOT *Jane, I have always trusted…*

> **Tip** Be careful when you describe places with *which* and *where*.
> - *which* / *that* replace a noun or pronoun:
>   *I grew up in the house (**which** / **that**) you're buying!*
>   (you're buying **the house**)
> - *where* replaces *there* or preposition of place + noun:
>   *I still live in the house **where** I grew up.*
>   (I grew up **in the house** / **there**)

9B Reported speech; reporting verbs

▶ 09.06

When we report what people said or thought in the past, we usually change the tenses, pronouns, possessives, and references to time and place:
*Anna: "I won't go out **tomorrow**."*
*Anna **told** me she **would** not go out **the next day**.*

present tenses ➜ past tenses
past tenses ➜ past perfect tenses
will, *can*, and *may* ➜ *would*, *could*, and *might*
Past perfect, *would*, *could*, and *might* don't normally change.

When the reporting verb is in a present tense, we don't change the tenses:
"I've never seen them in concert." ➜ *She **says** she's **never seen** them in concert.*

When we report questions, the word order is the same as in sentences. Use *whether* or *if* to report *Yes* / *No* questions. *Whether* is more formal than *if*:
"Where do you live?" ➜ *They asked me where **I lived**.*
NOT *They asked me where did I live.*
"Are you famous?" ➜ *They weren't sure if / **whether** I was famous.*

Reporting verbs

After some reporting verbs, there are different verb patterns:

Verb + (*that*) + clause	agree, assume, believe, complain, discover, find out, insist, promise, realize, say, state, …	He **stated that** he would stay with us.
Verb + sb + (*that*) clause	assure, inform, tell, warn, …	We **informed them that** it was ready.
Verb + *to* + infinitive	agree, promise, refuse, …	They **refused to speak** with us.
Verb + sb + *to* + infinitive	ask, order, remind, tell, …	She **ordered me to leave**.
Verb + gerund	admit, apologize for, deny, regret, suggest, …	He **admitted taking** the money.
Verb + (*sb*) + reported question	ask, discover, know, realize, wonder, …	I **wondered where they were**.

> **Tip** With negatives, use *not to* + infinitive or *not* + gerund.
> *We agreed **not to go**.*
> *He apologized **for not stopping** at the red light.*

150

9A Relative clauses

a Complete the sentences with the correct relative pronouns. If no word is needed, put (–).

1 This is my best friend, Kim, _____ I've known since we were little.
2 There are three things _____ I need to tell you about today's event.
3 Everybody congratulated the team, _____ hard work had won the contract.
4 The receptionist recommended the restaurant _____ we ate.
5 We never worried about money until the year _____ we bought our first house.
6 Who are the people _____ arrived late?
7 My job, _____ I love, is also really demanding.
8 They discovered a treatment _____ had no side effects.
9 I wish I could move to a seat _____ I could see out of the window.
10 The singer, _____ voice I have loved all my life, seemed to be singing directly to me.

b Correct one mistake in each sentence.

1 This is the book what I was telling you about.
2 There's a new machine at the gym I think you would really like it.
3 We're traveling to Dubai, where I've always wanted to visit.
4 I was worrying about my luggage, that I'd forgotten to weigh before we left.
5 Chris, who his father owns the company, always works really hard.
6 I've finally had to replace my old car, I've had since I passed my test.

c Rewrite the two sentences into one making all necessary changes to punctuation and word order. Remember to cut unnecessary words.

1 The band didn't come on stage until nine o'clock. They were supposed to start at eight-thirty.
2 The train company refunds passengers. The passengers' trains are delayed.
3 I looked in all the places. I thought I might have left my phone there.
4 The idea worked really well. We came up with the idea together.
5 Morocco is my favorite place for a vacation. We spent our honeymoon there.
6 The neighbors get back from vacation tomorrow. I'm looking after the neighbors' cat.

d ≫ Now go back to p. 106.

9B Reported speech; reporting verbs

a Look at the direct speech in the left-hand column. Complete the reported speech or thoughts in the right-hand column.

1 "I don't understand what you want." He told me _____that he didn't understand what I wanted._____
2 "Harry can't ski." I didn't realize _____
3 "You may feel a little sleepy after you take the pills." The doctor warned her that _____
4 "The exam will be really easy." I assumed _____
5 "No, I wasn't walking past the bank when I heard the alarm." The witness denied _____
6 "We've been trying to call you since we heard the news." They informed us that _____
7 "Margaret won't be happy when she finds out." I warned you _____
8 "I couldn't open the door because I'd forgotten my key." He discovered that _____

b Look at the questions from a job interview in the left-hand column. Complete the reported questions.

"What do you know about this company?"	They started by asking me [1] _____what I knew_____ about the company. Then
"Do you have any experience with this kind of work?"	they wanted to know [2]_____ any experience with that kind of work.
"How fast can you type?"	They even asked me [3]_____ type! Then I had to explain [4]_____
"Why did you leave your last job?"	my last job! The worst question was when they asked [5]_____ good at
"Are you good at dealing with customers?"	dealing with customers. They also wanted to know [6]_____ a team – I
"Have you ever managed a team?"	didn't know what to say! By the end, I wasn't sure [7]_____ for the job!
"Why have you applied for this job?"	

c Complete the reported speech, thoughts, and questions with **one** or **two** words in each blank. Contractions (e.g., *didn't*) count as one word.

1 "I promise that I'll be really careful." I promised __to be__ really careful.
2 "You must explain what you're doing here." The guard ordered _____ explain what we were doing there.
3 "Yes, OK. I told someone about the accident." Amanda admitted _____ someone about the accident.
4 "How did they find out?" I wondered how _____ found out.
5 "I'll pay for the meal – no discussion!" Robert insisted _____ for the meal.
6 "I'll send you a postcard." Sam told _____ send me a postcard.
7 "We're really sorry that we lost your order." They apologized _____ our order.
8 "OK, I can give you the money." Patricia agreed _____ us the money.

d ≫ Now go back to p. 108.

10A Past modals of deduction

We can use modal verbs to show that we are making a deduction, not stating a fact. We use the modal verbs *must, may, might, could,* and *can't + have +* past participle to make deductions about the past.

▶ 10.02

Deduction	Meaning
They are late.	I know for certain that they are late.
They are never late. They **must have gotten** lost.	I believe they got lost.
They **may / might / could have** gone the wrong way. They **might not have** found the right street.	I believe it's possible that they got lost.
They **couldn't have gotten** lost. They have GPS.	I believe they aren't lost.
They aren't lost. I can see them coming up the street now.	I know for a fact that they aren't lost.

The opposite of *must* for deductions is *couldn't.*

We can also use *may not have* or *might not have*:
*Try calling them at home. They **might not have** left.* (= It's possible that they haven't left yet.)

10B Wishes and regrets

▶ 10.08   When we make a wish, we imagine an unreal situation in the past, present, or future.

Wishes about the future	We use *would* to make wishes about the future. Don't use *would* to make a wish about yourself – use *could* instead.	*I **wish** it would stop raining.* *I **wish** I **could** get a better job, but I don't have enough experience.* (= if I had more experience, I would be able to get a better job.)
Wishes about the present	We can use the simple past to make wishes about the present. We can also make wishes about the present with *could +* infinitive.	*I **wish** I **had** more time.* (= I would like to have more time.) *I **wish** I **could** speak French – it's such a beautiful language.* (= I wish I was able to speak French, but I'm not.)
Wishes about the past	We use the past perfect to make wishes about the past.	*I **wish** I **hadn't been** so lazy in school.* (I was lazy when I was in school, and now I regret it.)

> 💡 **Tip**   To talk about something that we see as realistic, possible, or likely in the future, use *hope,* not *wish*:
> *I **hope** you get better soon.* NOT ~~I **wish** you would get better soon.~~

I wish … / if only …
If only … means the same as *I wish …,* and we use it in the same way.

> 💡 **Tip**   When making wishes about *I / he / she / it,* we can use *were* instead of *was. Were* is preferred in formal English, but in normal spoken English, both versions are common:
> *If only it **were** that simple.* (Or: … *it **was** that simple.*)

▶ 10.09   *should have +* past participle
We use *should have +* past participle to express regret about our own past actions:
*It's my fault. I **should have locked** the door.* (But I didn't lock it, so the burglars got in.)
*I didn't know she was sleeping. I **shouldn't have turned** the music on.* (But I did turn it on, so I woke her up.)

10A Past modals of deduction

a Complete the sentences with one of the phrases in the box and the correct form of the verb in parentheses. Use some of the phrases twice.

must have   may have   couldn't have   might not have

1 **A** We walked all the way home in the snow.
 B Wow – that ___must have been___ (be) cold!
2 **A** I think I saw Angela on the bus today.
 B No, it _____ (be) Angela – she's on vacation in the mountains this week.
3 **A** I saw a beautiful sweater in the store, but I didn't buy it. It's probably too late now.
 B Maybe, but let's go back and check – they _____ (sell) it yet.
4 **A** That's strange. My bicycle tire's flat. How did that happen?
 B I'm not sure. You _____ (ride) over some broken glass or something.
5 **A** Where have all the sandwiches gone? The plate's empty!
 B Tom _____ (eat) them. He was the only person who came into this room all day.
6 **A** I think I've broken my arm – it really hurts.
 B I don't know … you _____ (break) it. I'm not an expert, but it doesn't look broken.

b Check (✓) the correct sentences. Correct the mistakes.

1 ☐ I said hello but he didn't reply. He ~~didn't~~ have heard me.   _incorrect   must not_____
2 ☐ Sorry, I may not have made myself clear.   _____
3 ☐ I can't find my purse. Someone might stolen it.   _____
4 ☐ I don't know who wrote the report – it could had been anybody.   _____
5 ☐ They couldn't have just disappeared! It's impossible!   _____
6 ☐ It might haven't been such a good idea to walk home alone.   _____
7 ☐ They look sad. They must lose the match.   _____
8 ☐ Wow! That's a nice car! It needs to cost a fortune!   _____

c ≫ Now go back to p. 117.

10B Wishes and regrets

a Match the sentence halves.

1 ☐ Hmm … I don't like the look of those dark clouds.
2 ☐ I really regret leaving my old job.
3 ☐ I was sure the bank would lend us the money if we filled in a few forms.
4 ☐ It's really annoying that you told me the match result.
5 ☐ I don't know why they're so late.
6 ☐ I really miss you.
7 ☐ You never do any cleaning around the house.
8 ☐ It looks like a really nice place for a vacation.

a If only it were that simple.
b I hope nothing has happened to them.
c I wish you'd kept quiet about it.
d I wish you'd help out a little more.
e I hope it doesn't rain.
f If only it weren't so expensive!
g I wish I hadn't resigned from it.
h If only I could see you again.

b Write wishes or hopes for each of these situations. Use *If only*, *I wish*, or *I hope*.

1 Why didn't you remind us?   _____ _If only you'd reminded us._ _____
2 I don't know what to do.   _____
3 If I take this class, I might be able to speak Korean.   _____
4 They didn't warn us in advance, unfortunately.   _____
5 Maybe Ramón will help me.   _____
6 I'm angry that they canceled the flight.   _____

c Write sentences about these situations using *should have* + past participle. Use the words in parentheses.

1 Oh, no, we're going to be late. [leave home earlier]
 _____ _We should have left home earlier._ _____
2 I regret buying that new bag. It was too expensive. [not buy it]
 _____
3 I feel terrible after running so far. [stop earlier]
 _____

4 I really wanted to see that new movie and now it's too late. [go to the movies yesterday]
 _____
5 I went to a party yesterday. I didn't study. [not go to the party]
 _____

d ≫ Now go back to p. 120.

This page is intentionally left blank.

6A Travel and tourism

a Put the correct words from the box in the blanks. The definition of each word is given in parentheses.

feature   setting   structures   outskirts

1   … and there are waterfalls on the _____ of the city. (just before the city ends and the countryside begins)
2   However, the most amazing _____ you can see here is the nearby volcano, Parícutin. (an important thing that you notice)
3   … the whole island is like a museum of breathtaking wooden _____ that date from the 18th century. (things that you build)
4   In many ways it's the perfect _____ for them. (the position of a building)

b Match pictures a–f to examples 1–6 from a tourist guide.

1 ☐ Remember to tell your driver which **terminal** your flight's leaving from.
2 ☐ We also recommend a visit to the **studio** where he painted in the final years of his life.
3 ☐ We're both a hotel and a conference **venue**.
4 ☐ You can eat outside on our **patio**.
5 ☐ The lunch buffet is served every day between 11:30 a.m. and 2:00 p.m. in the room across from this **lobby**.
6 ☐ If you would like to go **hiking**, there are trails of different levels of difficulty.

c ▶06.08 Listen to Ana's story about going to Malaysia. Write the correct words in the blanks.
Last year we wanted to ¹_____ away for a week, so we decided to go trekking in the forests of Malaysia. We thought it would be cheaper to catch a train to the airport rather than go by taxi. But we were not happy to discover that the trains weren't ²_____ on time. We ³_____ at the check-in desk very late and barely managed to catch our flight. The flight took 17 hours because we ⁴_____ over in Dubai for a couple of hours. By the time we got there, we were exhausted and not really in the mood for trekking.

d 💬 Think about answers to the following questions. Then ask and answer them with a partner.
1   When you go traveling, do you usually arrive at the station or airport early or on time?
2   Imagine you have to go on a long flight from your country to another one. Where would you like to stop over? How long would you like to stop over for?
3   Have you ever been trekking? If yes, where did you go? If not, would you like to try?

PRONUNCIATION Consonant groups

a ▶06.09 Listen to the underlined sounds in these words. What do they have in common?

<u>st</u>udio   out<u>sk</u>irts   <u>str</u>ucture

b ▶06.10 Listen to these words. <u>Underline</u> where two or more consonants occur together in the same syllable.

approval   discussion   apply
hungry   transfer   contrast   destroy

c 💬 Write two sentences. Each sentence should contain at least two words from **b**. Read your sentences to each other.

d ⟫ Now go back to p. 70.

7B Movies and TV

a Look at the words in **bold** in sentences 1–8. Find two:
- words that refer to people who work in movies and TV
- verb forms that refer to when a movie or TV show is shown
- words that talk about the way TV shows are divided
- verb forms that talk about what can happen during the making of a TV show or movie.

1 The longest-running science fiction TV **series** is the British production *Doctor Who*.

2 As she walked through the front door, her look of complete surprise **was captured** on camera.
3 The first *Star Wars* movie **was released** in 1977.
4 After filming, the **editor** began the work of choosing the best shots and putting the movie together.

5 He appeared in only one short scene of the movie, but it **was cut** after filming finished.
6 Any big international sports event **is broadcast** live all around the world.

7 It's a really good news show because the **host** is completely neutral and you never know what her opinion is.

8 There's an exciting crime show on TV at the moment. Tonight is the final **episode**, and we'll find out who the murderer is.

b Answer the questions.
1 Does a TV series normally include more than one episode?
2 Viewers usually see a host on TV. Do they see the editor of a TV show?
3 When a movie is released, where do we usually see it, in a movie theater or on TV? Are news shows normally released or broadcast?
4 Who usually captures something on camera, an editor or a camera operator? Who cuts something?

c Are the four verb forms in **a** in an active or passive form? Is this form more typical for these verbs?

d Write words in the blanks. Use a word in **a** or from p. 84.
1 The _____ of the new comedy program is made up of actors who aren't famous.
2 The scene where he gets home has been _____. It's not necessary and it's pretty boring.
3 Every summer, a lot of big action movies are _____ because studios think they'll do well and make money.
4 Some people think the way a movie _____ puts together a movie is just as skillful as the work of the director.
5 The movie looked beautiful and was full of _____ of wonderful scenery, but the storyline and the _____ were terrible. I couldn't understand what was going on.
6 The Costa Rican TV show *Teleclub* is the world's longest running educational program. The first _____ was broadcast in 1963.
7 Having talked to the director about his ideas for the movie, the _____ felt enthusiastic and began thinking how he could get money to make it.
8 The accident was _____ on video by a member of the public using her phone.

e 💬 Discuss the questions.
1 What's a TV series that you've enjoyed recently? What's it about?
2 What kinds of things do you think shouldn't be broadcast live on TV?
3 What do you think is more important in a movie – a good script or great shots? Why?
4 Which job do you think would be the most interesting: producer, director, or editor? Why?

PRONUNCIATION Sound and spelling: *o*

a How many different pronunciations of the letter *o* are in the words below?

| c**o**nfirm | br**o**adcast | epis**o**de | t**o**gether | c**o**mpany |

b Which of the symbols and examples match the sounds in **a**?

Sound 1 /ɔ/	Sound 2 /u/	Sound 3 /ə/	Sound 4 /ʌ/	Sound 5 /aʊ/	Sound 6 /oʊ/
b**ou**ght	f**oo**d	c**o**nfess	m**o**ther	n**ow**	r**oa**d

c ▶ 07.07 Match the pronunciation of *o* in these words to the correct sound in **b**.
sh**ow** p**o**lice s**ou**ght y**ou**ng c**o**mmit
ch**o**se thr**ow** n**o**thing afterth**ou**ght

d 💬 Write two sentences. In each sentence try to use two *o* words that have a different sound. Read your sentences to each other.

e ≫ Now go back to p. 84.

8B Crime

a Read the two news reports. Match the pictures to the <u>underlined</u> words and phrases.

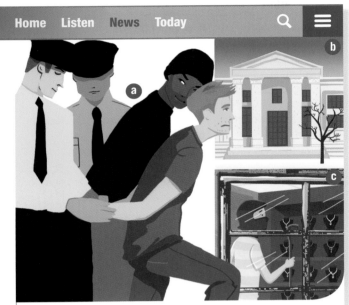

Home Listen News Today

Thieves [1]<u>broke into a jewelry store</u> and stole $5,000 worth of jewelery and watches. However, they were seen on CCTV, and [2]<u>two suspects were arrested</u> yesterday. They will appear in [3]<u>court</u> on Wednesday.

I saw her take money to the meeting.

We find her guilty.

We think you did it.

The [4]<u>trial</u> of Renata Rivers, who [5]<u>was accused of</u> theft, is finally over. It continued for over three weeks, and around 15 [6]<u>witnesses were called to give evidence</u>. Yesterday the [7]<u>jury gave a verdict of guilty</u>. The [8]<u>judge</u> <u>sentenced</u> Ms. Rivers to five years in prison.

b ▶ 08.07 Choose the correct words to complete the conversation. Then listen and check.

A Did you hear about the [1]*court / trial* of that company director?

B Oh, you mean the one who was [2]*accused / arrested* of bribery. I knew he'd been [3]*arrested / sentenced*. What happened?

A It was incredible. He appeared in [4]*trial / court* yesterday, and five [5]*suspects / witnesses* all gave [6]*evidence / verdicts*. They all said he had asked them for bribes.

B Wow. So, what was the [7]*verdict / trial*? Was he found [8]*accused / guilty*?

A No, the [9]*jury / witnesses* said he was not guilty.

B Hmm. What did the [10]*judge / jury* say?

A Nothing. She didn't [11]*arrest / sentence* him. She let him go free.

B Hmm. That's a little strange, isn't it?

c Think of a famous court case from your country or from a movie you've seen. Take notes on what happened. Think about:
- the crime and when it happened
- any suspects who were accused and/or arrested
- the trial and the witnesses who gave evidence
- the jury's verdict
- the judge's sentence.

d 💬 Discuss the court cases. Which one is the most interesting?

PRONUNCIATION Sound and spelling: *l*

a ▶ 08.08 Listen to the words. Is the letter *l* pronounced in all of them?

stole	talk
will	trial

b ▶ 08.09 <u>Underline</u> the word in each group where *l* is not pronounced.

1 called	could	cold
2 milk	incredible	walk
3 should	guilty	told
4 film	gold	half

c 💬 Practice saying all the words in **a** and **b** with and without the /l/ sound.

d ≫ Now go back to p. 97.

9A Health

a Match the texts to the pictures.

❶ "Last night I **bumped** my head against the kitchen cupboard door so hard that I collapsed on the ground and **lost consciousness**. I didn't cut myself badly, so I won't have a **scar**, but this morning there's a large **bruise** on my forehead."

❷ "A few months ago I woke up feeling very ill. My face was very **pale** and my head was **aching**. I also felt really **dizzy**. I went to the doctor and he said it was probably just an **infection**, so I stayed at home until I felt better."

b Match the words in **bold** in the texts to the definitions 1–8.
1 a temporary dark mark on your skin
2 to hurt part of your body by hitting it against something hard
3 when your face has less color than normal because you are ill
4 when you feel the world is spinning around
5 a more formal way of saying "pass out"
6 to have a continuous pain in a part of your body
7 a disease in a part of your body that is caused by bacteria or a virus
8 a permanent mark on the skin after you cut yourself

c Complete the sentences using the correct form of the words in **a**.
1 When I sit at my desk behind my computer all day, my back often starts to _____.
2 I almost _____ _____, so he poured cold water on my face to keep me awake.
3 I hardly slept last night, so now I feel exhausted and my face is _____.
4 I have a small car and I often _____ my head when I get in.
5 The _____ on my stomach is from an operation I had when I was a child.
6 He fell down and hit his leg on a chair yesterday. Now he has a big _____ on his knee.
7 My throat is very sore today. I probably have an

_____.
8 I always eat breakfast because if I don't, I usually start to feel _____ with hunger at about 11 o'clock.

d 💬🗣 Choose five of the words in **a** and **b** and tell a partner something that happened to you or someone you know, using the words. Ask and answer questions.

> I had an infection last month after I had a cold. I missed work for a week.

PRONUNCIATION Sound and spelling: *ui*

a ▶09.01 Put the words in pairs of the same vowel sound. Listen and check.

br**ui**se	q**uie**t
w**i**re	g**ui**tar
d**i**zzy	sh**o**es

b ▶09.02 What sound does *ui* have? Put the words in the correct box.

fr**ui**t	req**ui**re
inq**ui**re	g**ui**lt
s**ui**t	n**ui**sance
b**ui**ld	circ**ui**t
bisc**ui**t	acq**ui**re

Sound 1 /ɪ/	Sound 2 /u/	Sound 3 /waɪ/
guitar	bruise	quiet

c 💬🗣 Write three sentences. Each sentence should contain a *ui* word with a different sound. Read your sentences to other students. Check each other's pronunciation.

d ≫ Now go back to p. 106.

10A Adjectives with prefixes

a Read about William and his change of lifestyle. What part of his life does he change?

> William was working as a **legal** adviser. He was an **experienced** and **responsible** employee with **regular** working hours. But he was bored. He was not a **patient** man, either, and wanted to change his life before it was too late. So he handed in his notice and explained in a **formal** and **polite** manner that he was not **satisfied** with his situation.
>
> He then started working for himself as a gardener and discovered that it was even better than **expected**. He enjoyed working outdoors, he loved seeing all the wildlife around him, and he felt like a very **fortunate** man. He was happy that he had been **honest** with himself and followed his heart.

b Look at the adjectives in **bold** in the text. Add the opposite of the adjectives in the correct place in the chart. Use a dictionary to help you.

un-	in-	im-

ir-	il-	dis-

c Look again at the adjectives in the blog on p.118. Add them to the correct places.

d Complete these rules:

> We use *im-* instead of *in-* before adjectives beginning with the letter _____.
> We use *il-* instead of *in-* before adjectives beginning with the letter _____.
> We use *ir-* instead of *in-* before adjectives beginning with the letter _____.

e Use adjectives in the chart to complete the sentences.
1 Karen left top-secret documents in her car with the window open. It was very _____.
2 I inherited my grandmother's jewelry when she died. I had no idea she wanted me to have it, so it was completely _____.
3 Be careful of Alex. He may try to cheat you! He's pretty _____.
4 My sister always reads the last chapter first because she wants to find out what happens in the end. She's so _____.
5 I stayed in a hotel with terrible service. My friend recommended it to me, but I was very _____.

f 💬 Choose two of these questions and discuss them with a partner.
1 Do you ever get impatient? When?
2 What is the most unbelievable piece of news you've heard recently?
3 What's the most unexpected thing that's ever happened to you?

PRONUNCIATION Word stress

a ▶ 10.04 How many syllables do these words have? Put them in the correct place in the chart. Listen and check.

impatient	illegal
unfortunate	irregular
dishonest	inexperienced
irresponsible	dissatisfied

3 syllables	4 syllables	5 syllables

b ▶ 10.04 Listen again and mark the main stress in each word. Which two words also have a secondary stress?

c Where is the stress in all the 3- and 4-syllable words? What's different about the 5-syllable words?

d 💬 Choose three words with a different number of syllables. Say the word in a sentence to your partner. Check that your partner's stress is correct.

e ≫ Now go back to p. 118.

Phonemic symbols

Vowel sounds

/ə/ teach**er**	/æ/ m**a**n	/ʊ/ p**u**t	/ɑ/ g**o**t	/ɜ/ sh**ir**t	/u/ wh**o**	/ɔ/ w**a**lk
/ɪ/ ch**i**p	/i/ happ**y**	/e/ m**e**n	/ʌ/ b**u**t			

Diphthongs (two vowel sounds)

/eə/ h**air**	/ɪə/ n**ear**	/ɔɪ/ b**oy**	/aɪ/ f**i**ne	/eɪ/ l**a**te	/oʊ/ c**oa**t	/aʊ/ n**ow**

Consonants

/p/ **p**ill	/b/ **b**ook	/f/ **f**ace	/v/ **v**an	/t/ **t**ime	/d/ **d**og	/k/ **c**old	/g/ **g**o	/θ/ **th**irty	/ð/ **th**ey	/tʃ/ **ch**oose	/dʒ/ **j**eans
/s/ **s**ay	/z/ **z**ero	/ʃ/ **sh**oe	/ʒ/ u**s**ually	/m/ **m**e	/n/ **n**ow	/ŋ/ si**ng**	/h/ **h**ot	/l/ **l**ate	/r/ **r**ed	/w/ **w**ent	/j/ **y**es

Irregular verbs

Infinitive	Simple past	Past participle
be	was / were	been
become	became	become
blow	blew	blown
break	broke	broken
bring	brought	brought
build	built	built
buy	bought	bought
catch	caught	caught
choose	chose	chosen
come	came	come
cost	cost	cost
cut	cut	cut
deal	dealt	dealt
do	did	done
draw	drew	drawn
drink	drank	drunk
drive	drove	driven
eat	ate	eaten
fall	fell	fallen
feel	felt	felt
find	found	found
fly	flew	flown
forget	forgot	forgotten
get	got	gotten
give	gave	given
go	went	gone
grow	grew	grown
have	had	had
hear	heard	heard
hide	hid	hidden
hit	hit	hit
hold	held	held
keep	kept	kept
know	knew	known
lead	led	led

Infinitive	Simple past	Past participle
learn	learned	learned
leave	left	left
lend	lent	lent
let	let	let
lose	lost	lost
make	made	made
meet	met	met
pay	paid	paid
put	put	put
read	read	read
ride	rode	ridden
ring	rang	rung
run	ran	run
sink	sank	sunk
say	said	said
see	saw	seen
sell	sold	sold
set	set	set
sing	sang	sung
sleep	slept	slept
speak	spoke	spoken
spend	spent	spent
stand	stood	stood
steal	stole	stolen
swim	swam	swum
take	took	taken
teach	taught	taught
tell	told	told
think	thought	thought
throw	threw	thrown
understand	understood	understood
wake	woke	woken
wear	wore	worn
win	won	won
write	wrote	written

Acknowledgments

The authors and publishers acknowledge the following sources of copyright material and are grateful for the permissions granted. While every effort has been made, it has not always been possible to identify the sources of all the material used, or to trace all copyright holders. If any omissions are brought to our notice, we will be happy to include the appropriate acknowledgements on reprinting and in the next update to the digital edition, as applicable.

Key:
U = Unit, C = Communication, V = Vocabulary.

Text
U6: Guardian News & Media Ltd for the adapted text from 'Ancient tribal language becomes extinct as last speaker dies', by Jonathan Watts, *The Guardian, 10/02/2010.* Reproduced with permission; **C:** Extract from 'Separated twin boys with almost identical lives', *Reader's Digest.* Copyright 1980 Reader's Digest magazine. Reproduced with kind permission.

Photography
All the photographs are sourced from Getty Images.
U6: Fuse/Corbis; Museimage/Moment/Getty Images Plus; Westend61; PeopleImages/iStock/Getty Images Plus; Maskot; Salvator Barki/Moment/Getty Images Plus; Jose Fuste Raga/Corbis Documentary/Getty Images Plus; JORGE MURGUIA/500Px Plus; 12ee12/iStock/Getty Images Plus; Tsepova_Ekaterina/iStock/Getty Images Plus; Dinodia Photo/Corbis Documentary; MUJAHID SAFODIEN/Stringer/AFP; Boston Globe; Gallo Images - Emil von Maltitz/Riser/Getty Images Plus; Mihailomilovanovic/E+; Ciricvelibor/E+; GCShutter/E+; Mark Newman/The Image Bank; Prasit photo/Moment; Jane Khomi/Moment; RebeccaAng/RooM; www.sierralara.com/Moment/Getty Images Plus; Edb3_16/iStock/Getty Images Plus; Grant Faint/The Image Bank; **U7:** Philip Gould/Corbis Documentary; Grant Faint/The Image Bank Unreleased; Kevin Clogstoun/Lonely Planet Images/Getty Images Plus; Ben Stansall/AFP; View Pictures/Universal Images Group; Copyright Michael Mellinger/Moment; ©fitopardo/Moment Open; Lorado/E+; Caspar Benson; RuslanDashinsky/E+; M-gucci/iStock/Getty Images Plus; Robert Alexander/Archive Photos; Kritchanut/iStock/Getty Images Plus; Claire Doherty/In Pictures; Xuanyu Han/Moment; Ajr_images/iStock/Getty Images Plus; Marvin Fox/Moment Open; Yellow Dog Productions/DigitalVision; JohnnyGreig/E+; Jetta Productions Inc/DigitalVision; Luis Alvarez/DigitalVision; Zorazhuang/E+; **U8:** Tristan Fewings/Getty Images Entertainment; LightFieldStudios/iStock/Getty Images Plus; Maskot; Annabelle Breakey/Stone/Getty Images Plus; Rattanakun Thongbun/EyeEm; Laurence Mouton/Canopy/Getty Images Plus; BlackCAT/E+; Nicola Katie/E+; Funstock/E+; Deborah Feingold/Corbis Entertainment; **U9:** Jonas Gratzer/LightRocket; THOMAS SAMSON/AFP; Westend61; Andresr/E+; Massimo Ravera/Moment; EyeEm; Berlise De Jager/EyeEm; DaniloAndjus/E+; David Zaitz/The Image Bank; Kupicoo/E+; GlobalStock/E+; Stevica Mrdja/EyeEm; Reisegraf/iStock/Getty Images Plus; Patrickheagney/iStock/Getty Images Plus; Wingmar/iStock/Getty Images Plus; PNC/DigitalVision; **U10:** Michael H/Stone; Hulton Archive/Stringer/Hulton Archive; Sean Gladwell/Moment; Max Dannenbaum/The Image Bank; 104kelly/iStock/Getty Images Plus; Andrew_Howe/iStock/Getty Images Plus; STAN HONDA/Staff/AFP; Johnny Nunez/Getty Images Entertainment; Commercial Eye/The Image Bank; Cavan Images; Warrengoldswain/iStock/Getty Images Plus; Hill Street Studios/DigitalVision; Bokan76/iStock/Getty Images Plus; Tadamasa Taniguchi/Digital Vision; **C:** SebastiaanKroes/Moment; GUILLERMO LEGARIA/AFP; Devasahayam Chandra Dhas/iStock Unreleased; George Mathew/Moment; Sergei Bobylev/TASS; Anton Novoderezhkin/TASS; Justin Paget/The Image Bank/Getty Images Plus; Westend61; Sonatali/iStock/Getty Images Plus; DouglasPearson/Photolibrary/Getty Images Plus; Asbe/iStock/Getty Images Plus; DeAgostini/L.Romano/DeAgostiniPictureLibrary/Getty Images Plus; PATSTOCK/Moment; **V:** Hendrik Sulaiman/EyeEm; David Madison/Stone; Commercial Eye/The Image Bank.

The following photograph is sourced from another source/library.
U6: © FMGB Guggenheim Bilbao Museoa, 2020.

Cover photography by cdbrphotography/iStock/Getty Images Plus/Getty Images.

Illustration
QBS Learning; David Semple; Dusan Lakicevic; Gavin Reece; Jerome Mireault; Jo Goodberry; John (KJA Artists); Marie-Eve Tremblay; Mark Bird; Mark Duffin; Martin Sanders; Paul Williams; Roger Penwill; Sean (KJA Artists); Sean Sims.

Audio Production by John Marshall Media.

Corpus
Development of this publication has made use of the Cambridge English Corpus(CEC). The CEC is a computer database of contemporary spoken and written English, which currently stands at over one billion words. It includes British English, American English and other varieties of English. It also includes the Cambridge Learner Corpus, developed in collaboration with the University of Cambridge ESOL Examinations. Cambridge University Press has built up the CEC to provide evidence about language use that helps us to produce better language teaching materials.

English Profile
This product is informed by English Vocabulary Profile, built as part of English Profile, a collaborative program designed to enhance the learning, teaching and assessment of English worldwide. Its main funding partners are Cambridge University Press and Cambridge Assessment English and its aim is to create a "profile" for English, linked to the Common European Framework of Reference for Languages (CEFR). English Profile outcomes, such as the English Vocabulary Profile, will provide detailed information about the language that learners can be expected to demonstrate at each CEFR level, offering a clear benchmark for learners' proficiency. For more information, please visit www.englishprofile.org.

CALD
The Cambridge Advanced Learner's Dictionary is the world's most widely used dictionary for learners of English. Including all the words and phrases that learners are likely to come across, it also has easy-to-understand definitions and example sentences to show how the word is used in context. The Cambridge Advanced Learner's Dictionary is available online at dictionary.cambridge.org.

Shaftesbury Road, Cambridge CB2 8EA, United Kingdom

One Liberty Plaza, 20th Floor, New York, NY 10006, USA

477 Williamstown Road, Port Melbourne, VIC 3207, Australia

314–321, 3rd Floor, Plot 3, Splendor Forum, Jasola District Centre, New Delhi – 110025, India

103 Penang Road, #05-06/07, Visioncrest Commercial, Singapore 238467

Cambridge University Press & Assessment is a department of the University of Cambridge.

We share the University's mission to contribute to society through the pursuit of education, learning and research at the highest international levels of excellence.

www.cambridge.org
Information on this title: www.cambridge.org/9781108861434

First published 2022
20 19 18 17 16 15 14 13 12 11 10 9 8 7 6 5 4 3 2

Printed in Malaysia by Vivar Printing

A catalogue record for this publication is available from the British Library

ISBN 978-1-108-81719-6 Upper Intermediate Student's Book with eBook
ISBN 978-1-108-81730-1 Upper Intermediate Student's Book A with eBook
ISBN 978-1-108-81731-8 Upper Intermediate Student's Book B with eBook
ISBN 978-1-108-86138-0 Upper Intermediate Student's Book with Digital Pack
ISBN 978-1-108-86142-7 Upper Intermediate Student's Book A with Digital Pack
ISBN 978-1-108-86143-4 Upper Intermediate Student's Book B with Digital Pack
ISBN 978-1-108-81720-2 Upper Intermediate Workbook with Answers
ISBN 978-1-108-81722-6 Upper Intermediate Workbook A with Answers
ISBN 978-1-108-81723-3 Upper Intermediate Workbook B with Answers
ISBN 978-1-108-81724-0 Upper Intermediate Workbook without Answers
ISBN 978-1-108-81725-7 Upper Intermediate Workbook A without Answers
ISBN 978-1-108-81726-4 Upper Intermediate Workbook B without Answers
ISBN 978-1-108-81727-1 Upper Intermediate Full Contact with eBook
ISBN 978-1-108-81728-8 Upper Intermediate Full Contact A with eBook
ISBN 978-1-108-81729-5 Upper Intermediate Full Contact B with eBook
ISBN 978-1-108-86139-7 Upper Intermediate Full Contact with Digital Pack
ISBN 978-1-108-86140-3 Upper Intermediate Full Contact A with Digital Pack
ISBN 978-1-108-86141-0 Upper Intermediate Full Contact B with Digital Pack
ISBN 978-1-108-81732-5 Upper Intermediate Teacher's Book with Digital Pack
ISBN 978-1-108-81717-2 Upper Intermediate Presentation Plus

Additional resources for this publication at www.cambridge.org/americanempower

This page is intentionally left blank.

This page is intentionally left blank.